Fire & Wa

Fire & Water

The Power of Passion, the Force of Flow

Reg Lascaris & Mike Lipkin

ZEBRA

ZEBRA

Published by Zebra Press
a division of Struik Book Distributors (Pty) Ltd
(a member of the Struik Publishing Group (Pty) Ltd)
32 Thora Crescent, Wynberg, Sandton

Reg. No.: 63/06481/07

First published in September 1996
Second impression January 1997
Third impression March 1997
Second edition October 1997

Editor Hanneke Gagiano
Layout and cover design Neels Bezuidenhout

Reproduction by Disc Express cc, Johannesburg
Printed and bound by CTP Book Printers (Pty) Ltd, PO Box 6060, Parow East 7501

ISBN 1 86872 095 0

To magic, miracles and a sense of wonder

Contents

Foreword 1

I met Mike Lipkin for the first time one Saturday evening in September 1992, while I was browsing in a bookshop in the Hyde Park shopping centre. I remember him boldly coming up to me and introducing himself — 'Reg Lascaris, I presume?' he said rather than asked. 'My name is Mike Lipkin. It's a great pleasure to meet you. I really admire you and what you've achieved. I'd like to have a chat with you over coffee one day.'

I had heard of Mike before. At the time he was an account director at Ogilvy & Mather, an advertising agency. I sensed his energy immediately. I liked his directness and the open manner in which he approached me. On a whim, I asked him whether he would be interested in moving to Cape Town to manage our advertising agency there, which was without a managing director. Mike broke into a broad grin, shook my hand and turned me down. He told me he had just returned to South Africa from Canada, had bought a house and made his wife pregnant and that he was not yet ready to leave Ogilvy & Mather. On that note, we parted company, agreeing to see each other in the near future.

I next heard from Mike in January 1993. He phoned to tell me he had left Ogilvy & Mather and that he wanted to see me. I did a little checking of my own and discovered that he had actually been fired because of a difference of opinion between Mike and the Ogilvy & Mather directors. I agreed to see him anyway. When we met a few days later, Mike made a proposal that I couldn't refuse.

I have always loved people with *chutzpah*, that indefinable mixture of confidence, arrogance and cheek. Well, Mike Lipkin has *chutzpah* in spades. He offered Hunt Lascaris TBWA the opportunity to access his extraordinary insight and imagination on a retainer basis. He listed a dozen ways in which he would make Hunt Lascaris TBWA a better agency and suggested that the agreement start immediately. I smiled as Mike did his selling number on me. It didn't take me long to respond. After consulting with my colleagues, I gave Mike my answer. We didn't sign anything, we just shook hands. Our handshake was the start, not just of a rewarding business relationship, but of a deep friendship.

I don't know whether Mike has made Hunt Lascaris TBWA a better ad agency, but I do know that he has enriched me personally. There are certain people who have the ability to energise and enthuse the people around them. Mike has that effect on me. Every time we meet, I feel a little more charged and a little more excited about life. I think Mike magnifies my positive emotions. Our meetings are inevitably characterised by laughter, fun and the exploration of new ideas. No matter how much stress the two of us are under, our mutual delight in each other's company allows us to transcend the pressures of the moment. If you want to stay fresh and vital, make sure that you have at least one or two friends who have that effect on you. We all need a pick-me-up every now and then — and a human tonic is the best kind there is.

That was how our first book, *Revelling in the Wild: Business Lessons out of Africa*, originated. Mike called me one day to sound out the idea of co-authoring a book about business in the new South Africa. I had already co-authored two books with Nick Green, then managing director of Markinor, a research company. The two books were *Third World Destiny*, which was a marketing book aimed at highlighting new ways to segment South Africa's diverse population, and *Communication in the Third World*, which presented new guidelines for advertising to the South African consumer in the 1990s. Both books had become national best sellers. However, *Communication in the Third World* had been published in 1990, three years before. I was itching to write a new book. Mike's suggestion to co-author a book therefore struck a responsive chord in me.

Our objective in writing *Revelling in the Wild* was to outline a counter-convention form of business thinking integral to leading in the wild. South Africa is a wild country. It is a frontier society in the throes of rebirth. However, all the benchmark books on management being used by South African executives had been written in places like the USA and Britain. We set out to establish the new paradigms that should govern the way South African business people should think. In the process, we interviewed almost one hundred leading movers and shakers from every sector of South African society, including people like Raymond Ackerman, Andy Andrew, Robert Brozin, John Bryant, Pallo Jordan, Meyer Kahn, Richard Laubscher, Wendy Luhabe, Alex Molekoane, Jac Moolman, Jane Raphaely, Jon Qwelane and Peter Vundla.

The success of *Revelling in the Wild* vastly exceeded our expectations. It is now into its seventh printing, and has sold almost 20 000 copies. Although it was written at the end of 1993, the insights articulated in the book are even more relevant now than they were then. And, since I am an adman who can never resist an opportunity to sell anybody anything, I suggest that you read it if you haven't already done so.

In a way, *Fire & Water: The Power of Passion, the Force of Flow* is a sequel to *Revelling in the Wild*. It explores the discoveries about doing business in South Africa that Mike and I have made in the three years since *Revelling in the Wild* was published. But *Fire & Water* goes much further. It is not just about business mastery; it is about life mastery. It is an intensely personal book. We share our fears and flaws with you. We share our magic moments and our tragic moments. If one of the most important values of the new South Africa is transparency, we have tried very hard to be open with you, to take you into our world and into our minds.

Although *Fire & Water* is my fourth book, I am still amazed at the opportunity to communicate with so many people through the written word. In the age of the Internet, a book is still a very special phenomenon, something to be savoured like a fine wine or cognac. Co-authoring *Fire & Water* with Mike Lipkin has been an inspiring and learning experience for me. I hope that reading it will give you an equal pleasure.

REG LASCARIS
Johannesburg
August 1996

Foreword 2

In those immortal South African words, *Ek was diep in die kak* (I was in deep trouble). I had recently returned to South Africa after five years in Canada. Less than a year before, I had emerged from a prolonged battle with clinical depression. I was heavily in debt. My wife had just given birth to our third child. And I was unemployed, having just been fired. It was January 1993 and I had made up my mind to become an entrepreneur, mainly because I knew I was unemployable. I was scared as hell, but I was also strangely excited. I knew that I had a range of marketable skills, including sound marketing expertise, good presentation skills and a creative mind. The challenge, however, was getting anybody but me to believe that I did possess those skills.

Bad news travels quickly in Johannesburg village, especially in the marketing community. I knew that if I was going to survive, I needed just one high-profile client to give me business. I could then leverage that client to attract others. It is called validity by association. I did not have to think too long to decide which client should be my lifeline. It was Reg Lascaris. When I had met him fleetingly a few months before, I had sensed an immediate chemistry, and I felt that he was *simpatico*.

I called Reg to set up a meeting. I told him over the phone that I had left Ogilvy & Mather and that I wanted to speak to him about a mutual opportunity. 'Really?' he said sceptically, probing me in his inimitable manner. 'But I thought you were happy there?' I mumbled something about wanting to move on. There was a brief pause which I knew was Reg's way of telling me that he suspected the real reason for my departure. Then he said the magic words, 'When do you want to meet?' We set up a time for the following week and I spent the next ten days preparing for the most important meeting of my life. 'There is a tide in the affairs of men,' wrote William Shakespeare in *Julius Caesar*, 'Which, taken at the flood, leads on to fortune.' Well, my tide had just come in. My objective was to persuade Reg to put me on a retainer as a consultant to Hunt Lascaris TBWA. I intended to position myself as someone with the ability to deliver added value through unorthodox and audacious thinking.

As I walked into the Hunt Lascaris TBWA offices for the first time, I marvelled at the energy of the place. The atmosphere was crisp and cool, the white tile floors contrasting intriguingly with the indigenous African drums and artwork. As I observed the Hunt Lascaris TBWA staffers hustling and bustling about, I felt a sudden sense of loss. I knew that I would never work in an ad agency again. However, I could achieve the next best thing: I could become a consultant to one.

Jacqui Stark, Reg's secretary, came to collect me in the lobby and ushered me into Reg's office. As I entered, Reg rose to greet me. The impression I had formed of Reg when we had met four months before was reinforced. As I write these words, three years later, my opinion of the man has not changed. The best way I can describe Reg is that he is emotionally and intellectually taut. The crown sits uneasily on his head. It is as though his success has exceeded his expectations and that he lives in constant fear that someone or something might take it all away. It is that fear that drives him and that prevents him from ever being comfortable or becoming complacent. That fear is also what makes him so endearingly humble. He has the common touch: whoever you are and whatever you are, Reg will see you; he will speak to you; he will counsel you. He has never forgotten where he came from.

If listening is the most important part of the communication game, Reg is the game's grand master. He has the uncanny ability to become absolutely still as he single-mindedly focuses all his concentration on the person to whom he is speaking. I have observed this trait when Reg talks to me as well as when he talks to others. It is as if he is saying non-verbally, 'What you have to say to me is so important that I don't want to miss any of it. I am extremely interested in you.' I believe it is this trait — the ability to motivate people by making them feel special — that is at the heart of Reg's personal charisma. If this lesson is the only learning you take away from this book, its purchase price will have been worth it. However, Reg also demonstrates two more defining attributes of highly effective entrepreneurs: the ability not just to recognise opportunity but to intuit its presence and the ability to make quick and clear decisions.

I remember Reg smiling slightly as I made my proposal to him. It was a smile that communicated both amusement and affection. 'I'll get back to you,' was all he said. Within a week he did. 'You're in business,' he said to me over the phone, understanding the importance of his business to me. That was the beginning of the beginning. As I knew it would, my association with Reg attracted a range of other blue-chip clients. By March 1993, just two months later, I was running a thriving marketing and motivation company. All it took was a spark.

However, I knew that I needed something truly remarkable to differentiate me from the broad mass of marketing and motivation consultants plying their wares to an overtraded market. That something would be a best seller on doing business in the new South Africa — which I would co-author with Reg.

He responded enthusiastically to the idea when I suggested it to him. The gestation of the book took nine months (no coincidence). During that time, I spent countless hours with Reg as we ricocheted ideas and cross-pollinated insights off each other. Together, we interviewed almost 100 of the country's leading movers and shakers, many of whom are my most loyal clients today. The result was the bestselling *Revelling in the Wild: Business Lessons out of Africa*.

Revelling in the Wild awakened in me a passion to write. I discovered a magnificent satisfaction in articulating my thoughts in a way that would make other people want to read them. I also discovered that I could make a difference. So I decided to write a book on my experience with clinical depression, my subsequent recovery and the lessons I had learnt. I named the book *Lost and Found: My Journey to Hell and Back*. It was published in June 1994 and has already sold almost 20 000 copies. I call it the Coca-Cola of psychology books because it seems that almost all of us have lived in the dark shadow of life for at least a short period of time.

If *Revelling in the Wild* was about the new mindsets required for doing business in South Africa, and *Lost and Found* was about my personal odyssey, *Fire & Water: The Power of Passion, the Force of Flow* is about the beliefs, skills and desires that empower us to do truly great things. The spirit permeating the book is best expressed by Helen Keller when she said, 'Life is either a daring adventure or nothing!' As it is with everything I do with Reg, writing *Fire & Water* was an energising adventure. I hope reading it will be an adventure for you too.

MIKE LIPKIN
Johannesburg
August 1996

Introduction

What is it about fire that fascinates us so much? Why does it bewitch us? What is its intense attraction? Is it its energy? Its heat? Its brilliance? Its dance? Its crackle? Its power? Its ferocity? Its transience? Or is it that fire reflects our inner fire — the purity of passion that burns within us all?

And what is it about water that captivates us? Why do we find such comfort in its depths? Why do we want to be so close to it? Is it its constant current? Its rhythm? Its life force? Its purpose? Its motion? Its sound? Or is it that water resonates with our intrinsic flow — our own waves of emotion as they crash against life?

This book is the result of many animated discussions in front of the fireplace of both our homes. The fire that warmed us also seemed to heat up our dialogue. As we put on log after log, the fire renewed its energy and its flames burnt away our fatigue as we talked deep into the night. It was then that we decided fire is all about motion. Our fire within is what ignites us into action. As long as the flame blazes within us, we keep moving forward, sometimes against all odds.

But when it came to actually writing the book, when it came to crystallising our thinking into words, we needed water. Most of this book was written in houses overlooking either the Indian or Atlantic oceans. There is something about a huge body of water that calms and relaxes us and enables us to reach parts of our minds hidden to us in times of vigorous activity or acute emotions.

Fire and water, the two primal elements that are the essence of life — not just of the world around us, but of the world within. Our entire lives are spent trying to harness their disparate energy, trying to find a balance between passion and flow. And that is what this book is about — the middle path. The ability to apply the power of passion or the force of flow at the right time, to the right extent, for the right reason, in the right situation, with the right people.

This is an irreverent book about a highly relevant subject: how to lead ourselves and others so that we can enhance the quality of our own life and all those other lives that we have the privilege to touch.

We have written this book in the language we would use if we were having a one-to-one conversation with you. Both of us make a living through the ability to capture other people's imaginations. Everything we do depends on simultaneously informing and entertaining other people. We shall make you laugh as you read this book; we shall also make you cry. Do not be afraid to go with either emotion. In fact, if we could summarise our key message to you, it's this: Loosen up! Be you! Don't be afraid of anybody! Love the unknown and go boldly into the future, knowing you can handle anything that life throws at you.

We have designed *Fire & Water* as an interactive exercise and not as a monologue from us to you. We want to maximise your involvement because that is the only way in which you will truly internalise the experience. Throughout the book, we'll ask you to go within yourself and write down your thoughts, ideas and beliefs. Remember: the moment that you express your thoughts, you give yourself clarity and direction. In a sense, this book is simply a series of questions to which only you have the answers. We are merely your guides. There are no gurus. Everyone struggles with their own demons and everyone must find their own light. We hope that by asking you quality questions, you will find the solutions to your challenges. What's more, we would like to hear your opinions about the book. The feedback we received on *Revelling in the Wild* from hundreds of readers was invaluable to us. Write to *Fire & Water*, PO Box 41882, Craighall, 2024, South Africa.

If *Revelling in the Wild* was 'packaged optimism', then *Fire & Water* is 'packaged common sense'. We have written *Fire & Water* as a commonsensical handbook to help you master the everyday tests and trials that are part of every South African's life. It deals with real issues in a down-to-earth way. Neither of us is an academic. We have learnt our trade in the streets and sometimes in the gutters. This book is as much about heart as it is about what goes on in our heads. We offer you principles and techniques that can be applied immediately, no matter what you do or what rung on the human food chain you occupy. These principles and techniques are not just based on our experience: they are drawn from the highest achievers in South Africa and the rest of the world. They do not require an awe-inspiring IQ to be applied; they just require desire. Their impact lies in their simplicity.

Although this book has been co-authored, there are certain experiences or insights personal to each author. When we narrate these points we shall refer to the specific author in the third person, that is Reg or Mike. Many of the anecdotes related in the book are also sourced from the Power Talk series, a talk show on 702 Talk Radio hosted by Mike in which he interviews many of South Africa's movers and shakers. Most of all, though, this book was inspired by the passion and flow of the special breed of people living in the most exciting, scary, miraculous, untamed country on planet Earth — South Africa.

This book has been a hugely challenging joint venture between the two of us. Although we've known each other for four years, and have co-authored *Revelling in the Wild* together, *Fire & Water* highlighted our differences because it is so personal. Mike is almost pure fire. He is constantly burning with passion. Reg, on the other hand, is more laid back. He goes with the flow. He rows his boat downstream. The result of fire and water being mixed together, therefore, leads to some sizzling, steaming debates and to some equally hot ideas. In short, it leads to synergy. The two of us have created something that neither of us could have done alone. This also is our first message: celebrate your differences with others. Diversity equals creativity and breakthrough; conformity equals staleness and gridlock.

Before we start our journey together, we ask you to leave your baggage behind. Life is heavy enough. Where we are going, you will only need an open mind. As you move through this book, we know that there will be some points you really will respond to and some you won't. That's cool. Take what serves you and discard what does not. But be a participant, not just a critic. It is so easy to sit in the grandstand and watch life from afar, saying what you would have done had you been in charge. You are in charge. No matter what anybody else says, it is your life. So take charge.

Are you ready? Saddle up and let's get going.

One

Excitement: The spark of life

'You can't start a fire,
You can't start a fire without a spark,
This gun's for hire,
Even though we're all just dancing in the dark.'
— BRUCE SPRINGSTEEN, 'Dancing in the Dark'

How sensitive is your E-zone; your Excitement Zone? Before you proceed any further, consider these questions and scribble down your immediate response. Don't think too long on each issue; transfer your gut response to paper as it comes to you:

☛ How easily do you get excited?

. . . .
. . . .
. . . .
. . . .
. . . .

☛ What does it take to light your fire?

. . . .
. . . .
. . . .
. . . .
. . . .

☛ How much of each day do you spend in eager anticipation of what is going to happen next?

. . . .
. . . .
. . . .
. . . .

☛ Are you dependent on outside factors to produce a state of excitement within you, or do you ignite your own fire, irrespective of the weather outside?

. . . .
. . . .
. . . .

. . . .
. . . .

We believe that a person's performance at any given moment is directly related to their level of excitement. And we define excitement as a state of positive expectancy, a state where you are focused on an event or an experience that gives you pleasure, whatever your pleasure might be. We also like Webster's Dictionary's definition of excitement: 'the arousal or stirring up of emotions or feelings'. So answer these two questions:

☞ What can you think about right now that will give you immense pleasure (other than the obvious thoughts!)?

. . . .
. . . .
. . . .
. . . .
. . . .

☞ Why should you be excited right now? What is there in your life, big or small, to really turn you on? Even if you believe there is nothing, what could you be excited about if you really wanted to be?

. . . .
. . . .
. . . .
. . . .
. . . .

Excitement produces human electricity

Notice the surge in energy that comes from being excited. Feel the physical and mental change. If your E-zone is really developed, you are probably walking around with a permanent smile on your face. When we ask people how they feel when they are excited — such as when they have just received fabulous news or when they are anticipating fabulous news or a rewarding experience — they tell us that they feel powerful, alive, pumped up, that they can do anything. A woman told us she felt like Jean Claude van Damme when she was excited!

The absence of excitement, on the other hand, is the absence of energy. Just think about your capacity for vigorous activity, or taking yourself into the unknown without excitement. Feel the collapse of your personal power as you contemplate failure, boredom or, as we hear all the time, 'same shit, different day'. When we asked people how they felt when they had just received bad news or when they were especially pessimistic, they responded that they felt drained, paralysed, numb, tense, that they broke out into a cold sweat.

Notice your physiology when you are excited. Notice how you stand; notice how you walk; notice how you breathe; notice how you talk. Now think about your physiology when you are in a depressed state. Even our language reflects the difference. We describe someone who appears to be excelling with 'He's looking up.' On the other hand, we describe someone who is underperforming with 'She's looking down.'

We start this book with the issue of excitement because we believe that excitement is like electricity. Very little works without it. Like electricity, excitement can also be turned on and off at will, although most of us are not aware of this ability. Most people mistakenly believe that excitement is a rare commodity to be enjoyed only on special occasions, like birthdays. Although so much time is spent on equipping people with sales skills, presentation skills, management skills and technical skills, almost no time is ever spent on teaching people how to become excited, how to marshal their internal resources, or how to unleash their passion and personal energy without which nothing happens.

You can't give what you haven't got

The two of us attempt to spend the maximum amount of time possible in a state of excitement for one very important reason: we have no alternative. We are both here to inspire other people, to fill them with the energy to go out there and do great things. We understand one fundamental truth: *You can't give what you haven't got*. If you do not feel excitement, love, vitality, enthusiasm, joy, optimism or hope, you cannot give them to other people. We charge and recharge other people. If we permit ourselves to go slack, we take the positive tension out of the people around us. We are consciously aware of the need to sustain excitement; we consciously search for ways to motivate ourselves and others. Now consider your own circumstances. How different is your challenge from ours? Are you here to ignite other people's energy or do you depend on them to get your motor running? Are you conscious of the need to kindle the spirit of the people around you?

An advertising agency runs on human energy. It is a factory of the imagination, a place where ideas and concepts are designed and manufactured to stimulate desire. Nothing, absolutely nothing, happens without excitement and enthusiasm. Every day is a battle against the scourge of cynicism and mental fatigue. Every day is a search for the 'silver bullet': that breakthrough perception or view that will take the client's product or service to the next level.

As group managing director of Hunt Lascaris TBWA, Reg regards himself as jointly responsible for the vitality of his company: 'If my people look at me and see someone who has lost his enthusiasm or electricity, I know they may begin to doubt their own capacity to sustain excitement. I am aware that I am under constant observation by the people around me. In a way, I am one of the climate controls, not just for the people inside my company but also my clients. The majority of our clients invest over R5 million a year with us on advertising. And what are they really buying? Our ability to create added value through the superior communication of their products' personality, benefits and advantages. It is their ultimate expression of trust. They are literally putting their money where their mouths are. And it's up to us to keep reinforcing their trust, especially when the going gets tough. Because that's when they need the greatest assurance that the risks they are taking are worth taking. Our clients can sense our levels of energy and excitement immediately. It's not just the words we say, it's the level of commitment and passion behind the words.

'The foundation of Hunt Lascaris TBWA's achievements has been the team. We say you have to be a helluva individual to play on our team. But the entire team's performance rests on each and every player. The energy and excitement of each player directly impacts on the performance of the team as a whole.'

Mike, on the other hand, brands himself as South Africa's top peak-performance coach. In the year ending 31 July 1996, he delivered 251 talks/workshops — one every weekday, almost every week of the year. 'I cannot give in to my negative emotions. Every day, I am being paid to fire people up over a very short period of time. What's more, I don't have the luxury of taking time to warm up in a session. I have to hit the ground running. From the second I begin speaking or facilitating a workshop, I have to spark people.

'My toughest days are when I am running on empty, after I have been on the road for six to seven days at a time. I wake up in a strange place, disoriented and tired. I haven't seen my family for a week, I still have a headache from the night before and I have an eight-hour motivational session ahead of me. No one in the room cares about how many successful sessions I've completed. In fact, my previous successes have merely heightened their expectations. It's damn scary: I know that I cannot afford to deliver a mediocre session, not just for my own well-being but for the people who have privileged me by setting aside the time to listen to me. They have been looking forward to my session with great anticipation. I know I must do whatever it takes to delight them, irrespective of what's going on inside my head — because it's my purpose to excite people into action.'

We are not excited because we are succeeding, we are succeeding because we are excited

Now we know what you may be thinking. People say to us, 'It's all very well for you two guys to be excited. Just look at your lives. You are both involved in exciting industries and you're both leaders in your field. If we were in your position, we would also be excited. Who wouldn't be excited doing what you two guys are doing?' But our lives were not always this way. That is why *we are not excited because we are succeeding, we are succeeding because we are excited*. We have discovered that, like reading, writing or speaking, excitement is a learned skill. Excitement is a conditioning of the mind, a mental programming. Most of all, excitement is a way of interpreting life. We believe it is not what happens to you that is important, but how you represent what has happened to you in your own mind. What continually fascinates us is how differently people respond to the same events. Why is it that two people with the same level of intelligence, education and experience can be confronted with the same situation, but one of them moves into a state of excitement while the other is overcome with pessimism and fear? We see this phenomenon all the time. And we saw it within ourselves.

The Reg Lascaris story

'I emigrated to South Africa when I was four years old. My father was a banker. But like the cobbler's family who never have proper shoes, we never really had money. My father was a very cultured and educated man, but somehow I think he belonged to another time. He would have thrived in the Victorian era because his values, beliefs and style seemed to have been drawn from that period.

'Despite our lack of wealth, my father believed that education and upbringing were crucial to my development. He believed strongly in the lessons of history and he believed implicitly — to a fault, in fact — in the honesty and integrity of people. For my father, a handshake was everything. He lived by a code of honour that influenced everything he did. If he left me one legacy, it was that my word should always be my bond.

'Unfortunately, my father associated himself with people who didn't always share his code of honour. He was therefore let down and exploited a lot along the way. I don't think he had an understanding of the fierce cut and thrust of today's business environment. He believed in the old way of doing things. He changed careers frequently in an attempt to find his niche, but he never quite did. I remember us always moving. We never owned our own home, we were urban nomads. I landed up going to eight different schools, which is more than a little nerve-racking for anyone in their adolescent years. To make my life even more unsettled, I grew up separated from my mother because my parents were divorced. While we were moving restlessly from place to place, she was living in Johannesburg.

'After school, like so many other young guys, I really didn't have a clear idea of what I wanted to do or where I was going. So I registered for a B.Comm. at Wits. But I had no money and I sure as hell didn't have the grades to warrant a bursary. I looked around for part-time work so that I could attend varsity in the evenings. I started a small real estate agency with a friend. We called ourselves Young Homes because we were young, but everyone wanted to speak to Mr Young. We did sell a few homes, but it really wasn't a viable business in the longer term.

'By this stage, I couldn't afford my own place so I moved in with my mom. She lived in a small flat in Hillbrow. She was battling to make ends meet and I felt guilty about not being able to help her by contributing to her expenses. I remember feeling incredibly frustrated, especially when I looked at some of my wealthy acquaintances from the northern suburbs. I vowed to myself that one day I would get there. But I struggled to find direction. I also dropped out of university. I just couldn't motivate myself to do something that didn't light my fire. But you know what, I always had a dream of being a 'somebody'. I know it sounds like a line out of the movies, but it was a very real force within me. At that stage, my dream didn't have definition, but it did have power.

'I drifted into advertising and finally discovered a focus for my energy. I also discovered my true entrepreneurial spirit. I found out that I loved to sell. And I found people extremely interesting, especially the things that motivated them and the things that made them want to buy a product. I started to enjoy the high energy, interaction, pace and enthusiasm of the advertising agency environment. But like a lot of youngsters, I wasn't over-endowed with patience or discretion. I wanted to run before I could walk. So, what happened was that I naïvely became involved in starting an independent ad agency with some other partners. None of us knew anything about managing money, so we abdicated that task to someone who called himself an accountant. Well, you can imagine what happened… The accountant resigned one day, two days later I had a call from the bank, and three days later I was looking for someone to bail us out. I was shattered. I had incurred horrendous debt when I could least afford it. By this stage, I also had a wife and children. It's amazing how trouble seems to whack us when we least expect it. But it's also amazing what you can do when your back is against the wall: you know you have to go on and you have an undying passion to succeed. This desire, together with the solid support of my wife Maree and children, helped me beyond words.

'Over the next five years I settled down, took stock and learned a lot more about business whilst working for someone else. I guess this experience is an example of the cliché of attending the University of Life. But if you sustain your optimism and your desire to win, it's probably the best education you can get. I also learnt that there is a season for everything. I learnt that sometimes you just need to go with the flow. If you stay alert to life's opportunities, they eventually find you.

'My "once in a lifetime" opportunity happened in 1983 when I went into business with John Hunt (a copywriter) and Jenny Groenewald (an art director). We started our advertising agency and we called it Hunt Lascaris TBWA. It was second time lucky.

'Our first client, Neville Mackay, founder and chief executive of Kelly Girl, believed in us enough to give us his advertising account and some friendly business advice. We didn't earn any money for the first six months, but somehow we managed to stay afloat. The challenge and the dream were big enough to drive us through the first year. In fact, those were some of the most fun times we ever had. The big bite in the bum that used to get me into action every day was the frightening thought of ever failing again.

'Today, I'm still excited about the fascinating business of advertising and what I do. I'm 49 years old now and my objective is to die excited at 100.'

The Mike Lipkin story

'Unlike Reg, I am a second-generation South African. My grandfather emigrated to South Africa from Poland at the turn of the century to escape anti-Semitism. He had no formal education or skills, but he made a hell of a pickled herring. He ran a series of delicatessens in downtown Johannesburg for almost 40 years. My father was a chartered accountant who hated accounting. I think that's why he married an artist and dedicated his life to her work. My mother was the late Aileen Lipkin, one of South Africa's most celebrated artists and sculptors.

'My childhood was a privileged one. Although we were not that well off, I never lacked for anything. I went to a private school, King David, where I first discovered the rewards of real wealth. Many of the children in my class came from some of the richest families in South Africa. When I used to visit them,

I marvelled at the splendour of their homes. I made up my mind that one day I would live in one of those mansions. Money, status, power, recognition and material possessions were placed at the top of my private agenda, an agenda that would almost destroy me one day.

'Despite a stutter that plagued me throughout school, by the time I was in matric I knew that I wanted to get into advertising. It seemed like the perfect combination of art and business. I graduated with a B.Comm. from Wits and then completed my honours in marketing through Unisa while I was in the army. After a brief stint at Colgate Palmolive as a product manager, I joined Grey Phillips in 1982. At the time, Grey Phillips was South Africa's leading advertising agency. At Grey Phillips, I also discovered my role model: the agency's founder and chairman, Darryl Phillips. He had achieved everything I wanted to achieve. And so I cloned him. I walked in the same way, spoke in the same way, and even dressed in the same way as he did. It worked. I had learnt to fake it until I made it. In just five years I went from being a junior account executive to a director of the company responsible for almost R50 million worth of business. My earnings were commensurate with my achievement. At 28, I was almost in a position to fulfil my schoolboy aspirations.

'Then, in 1987, I emigrated with my family to Toronto, Canada, to see whether I could crack it in the North American market. And that's when I did my Humpty Dumpty act. After just two years I fell to pieces. I made a couple of disastrous financial decisions, which were the catalyst for a severe personal crisis. You see, until the age of 30 I had never screwed up. I didn't know what it was really like to fail. I had never really experienced a "hard knock". I could not deal with it. I became consumed with fear. My confidence deserted me. And I plunged into almost three years of depression. I was forced to return to South Africa where eventually I was literally shocked out of my despair through electro-convulsive therapy.

'I will never forget my feeling of excitement when I woke up the day after my final session of ECT. I couldn't believe my ability to feel happy after being depressed for so long. I swore to myself and my higher power that I would never take anything for granted again and that I would help others to do the same. I repeat that oath to myself every day. I do my best to walk my talk — and maybe that's why I am constantly excited.

'After my recovery, I worked at Ogilvy & Mather until I had a difference of opinion with the directors and was fired. In January 1993, I started my own company and called it Touch The Sky (Pty) Ltd, The Imagination Company. There were three main reasons why I chose that name: it expressed what I wanted to do every day; it was fun and unique; and any company that calls itself Touch The Sky (Pty) Ltd cannot take itself too seriously. At first, I thought that my activities would be purely related to marketing consulting. Then, in April 1993, my karma appeared in the guise of a magazine article on professional speakers. I was sitting in the waiting room of my dentist when I chanced across the story. I read that some of these speakers were earning more than R100 000 a month. I called one of the agents featured in the story, persuaded her to represent me and delivered my first paid talk in July 1993. Today, I can truly say I am living my dream. And this book is just another episode in my life's series. But I will never forget where I've been and how easy it was to get there. I know that my antidote to depression is excitement, or rather, the decision to focus on why I should be excited.'

A crisis is a gift

There is a wonderful parable that expresses the key lesson we have learnt on our life's journey so far. Once upon a time in a far-off land there lived a man called Ahmed. Ahmed's pride and joy was a magnificent black stallion. This stallion was not only Ahmed's most treasured possession, it was also his means of making a living. Neighbours from miles around used to bring their mares to Ahmed to be 'covered' by his stallion, and they paid a hefty fee for the privilege of doing so. 'You are so lucky,' they said to Ahmed. And Ahmed replied, 'Maybe and maybe not.' Then, one day, Ahmed's stallion disappeared. His neighbours came to him and said, 'Ahmed, this is terrible news.' And Ahmed replied, 'Maybe and maybe not.' Two days later, Ahmed's stallion reappeared with two other magnificent stallions it had befriended while wandering in the desert near where Ahmed lived. 'This is wonderful news!' Ahmed's neighbours cried. 'Maybe and maybe not,' was his response. Now, Ahmed had a son who loved horses. He mounted one of the new stallions and was immediately thrown by the wild horse. As he fell, he broke both his legs. 'This is terrible news!' the neighbours wailed. 'Maybe and maybe not,' was Ahmed's response. The following week it was announced that a neighbouring state had declared war on Ahmed's country. The government, desperate for troops, was rounding up all the young men it could find, but it couldn't take Ahmed's son because his legs were broken. 'You are so lucky!' his neighbours cried in unison. And what was Ahmed's response? You guessed it.

What Ahmed knew — and what took us a lifetime to discover — is that truly effective people do not allow what is going on around them to dictate their inner state. They are masters of their own emotions. They carry their own weather within because they know that everything that happens to them has value. Even the most adverse experiences can be a lesson — if we search for the learning it represents. Think about when you have genuinely grown as a person or as a professional. Was it when things went smoothly? Was it when you had received fantastic news? Or was it when you had been confronted with a situation you weren't quite sure you could handle — a crisis, in other words?

We believe crises are gifts. They are given to us to stretch our capacity to manage stress. Crises are actually camouflaged possibilities for growth. So the next time you feel that you are going through a crisis, become excited! You are about to break through to the next level. We don't believe that there is such a thing as a learning curve. Life is far too volatile and unpredictable for that. Rather, we believe in learning breakthroughs. Life is either a series of upward steps — periods of plateaux interrupted by insights and learning that take us to the next level until our next insight takes us to the next level, and so on — or life is a neverending cycle of despair where every adverse experience simply reinforces our feeling of helplessness. It all depends on the meaning you assign to your experience. The next time you find yourself experiencing a 'crisis', focus on how life is serving you, not on how life is victimising you.

The story of how Thami Mazwai, editor of *Enterprise* magazine, passed his matric dramatically illustrates the power to squeeze maximum value out of even the most severe crisis. Thami told his story to Mike on Power Talk on 702 Talk Radio: 'When I was arrested in 1963, I was a matric student at Orlando High. But I didn't pass because of all the political unrest and my political activity as a member of the PAC. I was sentenced and sent to Kroonstad Prison where I was not the best behaved of prisoners. However, while I was there I made up my mind to pass my matric. Well, it was quite a traumatic process. I first had to apply for permission to study, then my application took about three months to process. After that I had to get my people to send me money to pay for the correspondence course. I had to do hard labour during the day and study at night. One day, though, the commanding officer approached me and told me that I was *"'n boompie wat nie wil buig nie"* (I was a small tree that wouldn't bend). He told me he had a better place for me and by that he was referring to Robben Island. And that's where I was sent. When I arrived at Robben Island, the whole process of applying for permission to study had to start all over again. I eventually received permission to study a month before I was supposed to write my matric examinations. But Robben Island really was a university in its own right. For example, Dennis Brutus, one of South Africa's leading poets, was in the cell next to mine. He taught me English and other prisoners taught me the rest of the syllabus. And guess what — I passed my matric.'

Before you read any further, think about what your response would have been if you had been in Mazwai's situation.

The more you take for granted, the less excitement you experience. The less you take for granted, the more excitement you experience

An excited mind is an enquiring mind. It is a mind that constantly challenges the status quo with the possibility question: 'What if?', and not the tired defeatist response of 'What for?' Mzwake Mbuli, the 'people's poet' and the man who presented his poetry at the inauguration of President Mandela, shares his spirit of excitement: 'Even when I was a child, I became excited when I questioned why things were the way they were, and how they could be changed. I used to question why cars actually keep to the left-hand side of the road and not the right; I used to look at the calendar and wonder why there are 30 or 31 days in the month and why not 35 or 40; I used to look at the emblem in the old Vierkleur flag and wonder why it didn't include my favourite dish; I looked at the continent of Africa and wondered why it was the shape of a question mark. I think it is because we have to question everything.'

However, if you really want to come face to face with pure excitement, spend as much time as you can with kids under the age of eight. Have you ever noticed how everything excites them? Have you noticed their immunity to cynicism and boredom? Have you really appreciated their incredible insight and wisdom? When you finish this book, read a wonderful book called *Children's Letters to God*. The book contains illustrated letters that kids between the ages of five and eight wrote to God. Here's a sample:

Dear God, I read your book. Where do you get your ideas?

Dear God, are you rich or just famous?

Dear God, why don't you leave the sun out at night when we need it most?

Dear God, do plastic flowers make you mad? They'd make me mad if I made the real ones.

Dear God, I didn't think orange went very well with purple until I saw the sunset last Tuesday. That was cool.

Dear God, you should only let very good friends get married. The neighbours fight all the time.

Dear God, I know you are supposed to love thy neighbour but if Mark keeps taking my skate, he's going to get it!

So what does it take to get you excited? Do you have to win the lottery? Do you have to get a major promotion? Do you have to take that overseas vacation? Do you have to meet the lover of your dreams? Or do you just have to wake up in the morning? What are your rules for getting excited? Here are some of the things that get us excited:

- ☞ Every time we receive a thank you.
- ☞ Every time we witness a flawless Gauteng sky.
- ☞ Every time we witness the clouds crowning Table Mountain.
- ☞ Every time we watch the sun dip into the ocean off the beach at Camps Bay.
- ☞ Every time we hear a hyena laugh as we sit round a campfire in the bush.
- ☞ Every time we smell the thatch of the rondawels in the Kruger National Park.
- ☞ Every time we hear, taste or feel something beautiful.
- ☞ Every time we sip a single-malt Scotch after a brutal day's work.
- ☞ Every time we smile or are smiled upon.
- ☞ Every time we laugh or make other people laugh.
- ☞ Every time we make it home at the end of the day without being hijacked.
- ☞ Every time we learn something new.
- ☞ Every time we inspire someone else to learn something new.
- ☞ Every time we read about an ordinary person who has done the extra-ordinary.
- ☞ Every time we see what gorgeous people our kids are becoming.
- ☞ Every time we succeed at something we haven't done before.
- ☞ Every time we fail at something we haven't done before.
- ☞ Every time we do something that we are proud of having done.
- ☞ Every time we meet someone who is even more excited than we are.
- ☞ Every time we think about how far South Africa has come in the past three years.
- ☞ Every time we read good news about South Africa.
- ☞ Every time we see the new South African flag.
- ☞ Every time we go overseas and are celebrated as South Africans.
- ☞ Every time we sell just one more book.
- ☞ Every time we hear that someone has actually read our book.
- ☞ Every time we get great service from the air crew on SAA.
- ☞ Every time we win a new client or assignment.

If we've learnt one thing, it is that excitement and gratitude are twin emotions. The more you take for granted, the less excitement you feel. The less you take for granted, the more excitement you feel. We've both tasted the bitterness of failure and frustration. We've both created whatever we have out of nothing. But what we both work very hard at is to not forget where we have been; to not become complacent or blasé about where we are; to not lose our sense of wonder, no matter how big the problems confronting us appear to be.

Beware of the AAK

Human beings have an infinite capacity for taking things for granted. We have a pathological need to bitch about something while ignoring the wonders that life has given us. That is when we receive an AAK from above. The AAK is an Attitude Adjustment Klap to remind us of what is really important. Throughout the biographies of high achievers going back 500 years, there is a prevailing theme: it often takes a life-threatening event or illness to remind us of the specialness of life. It is only when life is almost taken away from us that we recognise and appreciate its magic. Just before he died of cancer at age 52, Michael Landon, the well-known American actor of 'Little House on the Prairie' fame, said, 'Someone should tell us that we are busy dying when we are born, because then we would really appreciate life!' Every day is your life in miniature. How you live today will determine what happens to the rest of your life. Yesterday is gone forever, tomorrow does not exist yet. Today is a gift. Why do you think they call it the 'present'? So, don't wait for your personal AAK — get grateful now. Life is too short not to become excited.

How to become excited by really trying

Excitement has many close relatives. These are the emotions that turn up the dial on the pleasure we get from life. We have already spoken about one of these emotions — gratitude. By actively going for the following feelings, we make it easier for ourselves to become excited:

Love: Consciously look for ways to love the people and things around you. Love means always looking for the best in people. It motivates you to give. It is also your vaccination against intolerance, irritation and prejudice. It is your first-class ticket to excitement.

Curiosity: Be curious about everything. The quality of your life depends on the quality of the questions you ask. Every successful person we know is a curious person. They absolutely love learning. Ask yourself the following questions continually and you'll soon find yourself in a constant state of excitement: 'What if?' 'Why not?' 'How about?' 'Why don't we?' 'Why do you?' 'Imagine?' 'How can I use this?'

Determination and commitment: These are the twin emotions of strength. Determination is really perseverance in the face of adversity. Commitment is the pledge we make to ourselves that makes us determined. When you commit yourself to something, you eliminate all possibility of not following it through. Together, determination and commitment are the bridge over troubled water. They give us the ability to anticipate the pleasure through the pain. Without them, you can never sustain excitement. But most people are what we call 'early settlers'. They settle for whatever life gives them. They fail to break through the barriers that life puts in front of them, unaware of the magic that remains hidden from view nearby.

Adaptability: As the world changes and as you grow, change your beliefs and values accordingly. Inflexibility is the enemy of excitement and the handmaiden of fear. If you are adaptable, you are always experimenting; you are always trying something new; you are an explorer.

Confidence: Confidence is really inner security. It is the feeling that you can handle whatever happens to you. It is an emotion we can cultivate within ourselves. Without confidence, you cannot become excited because you are uncertain about your ability to seize the opportunities that may come your way. Listen to Nike when they tell us to 'Just Do It'. It's ready, fire, aim. We become confident by constantly taking action, by making things happen, not by watching things happen: if all you do is watch, eventually you will wonder what happened.

Consciously get in touch with your inner wolf

One of the best movies we have seen is 'Wolf', starring Jack Nicholson and Michelle Pfeiffer. In the movie, Nicholson plays the role of a tired, 58-year-old publishing executive who has just been manoeuvred out of a job by a younger colleague. Then, one night on his way home during a snowstorm, he runs over a wolf that is crossing the road. Nicholson gets out of the car to check whether the wolf is alive or dead, and is bitten by the wolf. The transformation of Nicholson is dramatic: he is invested with the energy of the wolf; he becomes youthful, vibrant, ferocious and robust. His senses become acute: he can smell the liquor on a man's breath from 50 metres away; his hearing is greatly amplified; he can bound up 20 steps in a single leap; his mind becomes razor sharp; and, of course, his libido becomes so powerful that Michelle Pfeiffer is mesmerised by him.

In an attempt to discover what is happening to him, Nicholson consults an ancient Indian mystic. After listening to Nicholson's story, the mystic tells him that the bite of the wolf awakened the wolf that was slumbering within him.

Just like Nicholson, we all have an inner wolf that may be hibernating, denying us his energy. Treat this book as your wolfbite and go howl at the moon the next time it's full. A little wildness can go a long, long way.

Excitement is contagious; passion is persuasive; and selling is first and foremost the transfer of enthusiasm

So what are we really saying to you? We are saying that you can get into a state of excitement simply by focusing on those experiences, things or people that make you excited or grateful. It is not easy. It takes practice, relentless practice. But eventually it becomes a habit. Eventually, you discover that 'reality' is not something 'out there', reality is something inside your head and your heart. People often ask us how come we are always so positive. Simply, what we have discovered is that we have a choice. We can decide whether to be excited or depressed. Well, we have both spent time in life's pits. We both remember what it was like. We have also flown with the eagles. Flying with the eagles is better. So we choose to exercise our choice, our choice to be excited, passionate, joyful, playful and wonder-full.

Do you interact with other people every day? Are you in sales or marketing (aren't we all)? Are you a manager or leader of others? Would you like to influence people to accept your point of view? Then consider these fundamental truths:

☞ Excitement is contagious.
☞ Passion is persuasive.
☞ Selling is first and foremost the transfer of enthusiasm.

You see, people want to be with people who make them enthusiastic, passionate and excited. We don't buy products, services or skills. We buy states, specifically states of happiness and pleasure. We buy people who have the ability to lift us up. Look around you. Who are the people who appear to be excelling? Are they not the people who are consistently exciting other people? Makes you think, doesn't it?

You can flick your excitement switch anytime you want to

Once upon a time, there was a little boy who lived with his family in a little house on the edge of a forest. One drizzly, overcast day, as he was walking home through the forest, he saw a little gosling dragging itself through the mud, its left wing hanging uselessly at its side. He gently picked up the tiny creature and took it home to his mother. After examining the wing closely, his mother saw that it was broken. She made a small splint for the broken wing. Then she prepared a nest of warm blankets for the gosling. Within a couple of weeks, the gosling's wing had healed. The family decided to adopt the gosling as their pet. The father built a shelter for the gosling in the family's backyard. The family showered the gosling with love and affection.

Over the next two years, as the gosling grew into a fine, healthy goose, it was happy. It had everything any living creature could have wanted. But by the time this goose was four years old, it had become clinically depressed. Every day, it would walk from one side of the backyard to the other. It would have to eat the same food, it would see the same things; but the goose instinctively craved the company of other geese. Slowly, its spirit died until it just lay in its shelter without moving, week after week, month after month, year after year.

So why did this goose get so depressed? The answer is simple: the goose did not know that it could fly! Just like the goose, people often live their lives in ignorance of their ability to fly on the wings of their imagination. You can flick your excitement switch anytime you want to. You excite yourself by simply thinking about what makes you excited.

Try this exercise right now: think of a great experience you have had in the past six months (come on, there must have been at least one!), or think of someone whom you really love or lust after, or someone who really loves or lusts after you, or think about something you can look forward to in the next six months. Or think about anything you really have to be grateful for. Or think about any reason why you should be happy — or could be happy — right now. Get this motivating image in your mind, sharpen it, brighten it, enlarge it. Savour it. Let it envelop you. Live it. Now get another image and another and another. Practise living in the mental reality you want to create for yourself. This is not brain surgery. It doesn't require the IQ of an Einstein. Anyone can do it: you just have to become aware of your power to excite yourself.

It is not natural never to feel down; it is impossible to always be happy in the face of the brutal facts of life in South Africa

Before we move on to the next chapter, we'll address one issue that we know you are thinking about because people always raise it with us: *it is not natural never to feel down; it is impossible to always be happy in the face of the brutal facts of life in South Africa*. We agree. Never to feel down, to ignore the pain, to pretend that nothing hurts is to live in denial (and that's not a place in Egypt). We believe that the challenge is fourfold:

☛ Firstly, we need to feel the pain without allowing it to scar us emotionally. We have to learn how to prevent ourselves from becoming cynical so that we don't have to feel that pain again. Think about what it means to be cynical. It means anticipating the worst so that you can never be disappointed. Cynicism is the direct opposite of excitement. It is impossible to be both cynical and excited at the same time. Webster's Dictionary describes a cynic as a person who believes that only selfishness motivates human actions. We define a cynic as someone who smells flowers and immediately looks for the coffin. If you are a cynic, you are condemned to a life of misery and depression.

Our message to you is: *Do not attempt to avoid the pain.* You can only heal what you can feel. Pain and pleasure are Siamese twins, they are inextricably linked. A person who feels no pain, feels no pleasure. Such a person lives in the emotional twilight zone. Did you know that one of the most common symptoms of clinical depression is an emotional numbness, an inability to cry or laugh? Grief, on the other hand, is when you open yourself to sorrow and move through it. You accept it and, eventually, you leave it behind you.

☛ Secondly, we need to learn from the pain; to receive the message it is sending us; to apply a positive interpretation to the event, not to regard it as a curse or demonstration of life's cruelty and unfairness. In his book *Learned Optimism*, Martin Seligman talks about our 'explanatory style'. By this he means the style we have of explaining the reason why things happen to us, and the meaning of those experiences. He says that optimists have an explanatory style that serves them. They never regard themselves as victims; they explain every event to themselves in a way that serves and motivates them.

☛ Thirdly, we have to accelerate the time it takes to recover from our psychological or emotional wounds. The fitter the athlete, the quicker the athlete recovers from physical injuries. The more developed your emotional muscles become, the more rapidly you recover from life's blows. That is why, throughout this book, we ask you questions designed to strengthen your emotional toughness. Think them through, act on your answers, come back to them again and again. *Fire & Water* is really a series of emotional and psychological aerobics sessions.

☛ Fourthly, we need to forgive ourselves for feeling down. There are times when we have to go with the flow, to indulge in our emotions without feeling guilty or weak. It takes guts to cry, especially if you're a man. It takes real courage to come face to face with your vulnerability and to accept its momentary mastery over you. In those times we need to take time out until we feel strong enough to get back into the fray. No one, not even Mike Lipkin, can live in excitement all the time. However, when we are down, we need to find the quiet and the calm, not the panic or the anxiety. It is during our down time that we either prepare ourselves to climb to the next level or that we relegate ourselves to a lower level by worrying ourselves to exhaustion.

What is the biggest obstacle to excitement? What inhibits our passion and interrupts our flow?

Two

Fear:
Friend or foe?

It is time to come face to face with the F-word. It is time to come face to face with the bundle of emotions we package under the label of *fear*. Before you proceed any further, take a few moments to consider these questions and write down your response:

☛ What are your three greatest fears?

....
....
....
....
....

☛ What would you really like to do right now if you weren't so scared to do it?

....
....
....
....
....

☛ Do your fears paralyse you or do they prod you into action? Why?

....
....
....
....
....

☛ When you feel the fear, do you feel as though you shouldn't be feeling the fear?

....
....
....
....
....

☛ What three real-life situations would you do almost anything to avoid?

....
....

. . . .
. . . .
. . . .

☛ If you did what you are most afraid to do, would it improve the quality of your life? How?

. . . .
. . . .
. . . .
. . . .
. . . .

☛ Which of the following emotions have you experienced in the past three months, and what action did you take as a result of experiencing them?

worry . . . .
. . . .

panic . . . .
. . . .

hurt . . . .
. . . .

anger . . . .
. . . .

frustration . . . .
. . . .

disappointment . . . .
. . . .

rejection . . . .
. . . .

guilt . . . .
. . . .

inadequacy . . . .
. . . .

feeling overwhelmed . . . .
. . . .

confusion . . . .
. . . .

loneliness . . . .
. . . .

vulnerability . . . .
. . . .

pessimism . . . .
. . . .
despair . . . .
. . . .
resignation . . . .
. . . .
sadness . . . .
. . . .
failure . . . .
. . . .

Burnout — what happens when fear gets out of control

You feel as though you are walking along the edge of the precipice. Moving forward is like trying to walk with heavy weights attached to each shoe. Each step is difficult and thinking of the entire journey fills you with panic. You are overdosing on adrenalin. Your heart rate is accelerating. Your breathing quickens. Your blood is being redirected to the heart, lungs and muscles. The chemical cortisol is being released to thicken the blood so that it clots more easily. Hydrochloric acid is pumping into your system. Digestion is slowed. The liver increases the level of glucose in your blood. Your body is screaming *NO!! Stop this stressful event!* But you cannot. There is no way out.

Day after day, week after week, the stress forces you into fight-or-flight mode. But you can't fight it and you can't flee. The arteries in your heart are being physically impaired. Your immune system is becoming more vulnerable. You find yourself succumbing to sickness more often. Endorphins, the body's natural anaesthetic, flow less readily. You feel pain more intensely.

Physically, mentally, emotionally, you are exhausted. You are feeling cut off from people. You achieve little, despite squeezing out the last drops of remaining energy. Life is a blur. You are capsizing in the permanent white waters and there is no lifeline. You are experiencing the final response to cumulative, long-term negative stress. You are suffering from burnout. Like a termite from hell, burnout bores right into you, eating your self and your soul away.

Burnout is a jargon word specifically used to describe the stress that people in the workplace feel when they are under tremendous pressure and cannot cope. But burnout in the workplace burns you out in every facet of your existence. It is when your fire is raging out of control. It leaves you going home at night with nothing left to contribute to family life. You feel helpless and hopeless. You feel guilty. The many things to do and roles to perform are tearing you apart. The only light at the end of the tunnel is an oncoming train. Your mother never told you that there would be days, months, even years like this!

You may try to alleviate your problems in self-destructive ways: excessive drinking, overeating (or in psychological parlance, comfort eating), smoking heavily, sniffing the white stuff, relying on anti-depressants or tranquillisers, failing to deal with difficult issues or procrastinating as long as possible. Sound sickeningly familiar?

But in a wonderfully perverse kind of way, burnout is the new common bond that is binding us together in the new South Africa. In the spirit of the times, it is unflinchingly democratic. If there is any justice in the world, it is that the people at the very top of the socio-corporate pyramid are suffering as intensely as the great mass of people at the base. The only difference is that you eat better at the top. In fact, the irony of burnout at the top is that wealth simply equips people to destroy themselves more expensively.

Burnout is the price of achievement. It is the price paid by the conscientious who keep going despite their private hell. This applies to us and we know it applies to you, because we know that the people who buy our books are strivers, achievers who keep pushing themselves harder and harder. Like us, you have probably tried to carry on with decreasing effectiveness at times, attempting to compensate by dragging even more strength from your rapidly depleting stock. Anxiety becomes your constant, unwelcome companion. Even in your quieter moments, the everpresent undercurrent of irritability disturbs your peace of mind. But still you force yourself to cope. You are one of the modern-day South African heroes. But the precipice looms ever larger and more terrifying, and there is no reassuring cord tied around your ankles that will break your fall into the abyss.

The problem is even worse for men than women, says noted industrial psychologist, Denise Bjorkman. 'Men tend to inhibit their emotions. They're not as expressive as women. They hide their pain. They deny their pain. Although women are subject to even greater stressors than men because of the multiplicity of roles they must play, their coping skills are better developed. She is much more verbal. She ventilates more. She cries when she needs to cry. She will see a psychologist if she has to. Although burnout is as real to her as it is to him, her biological destiny and ego structure do not depend on being leader of the corporate pack. And even when she is the sole breadwinner, her womanhood is not threatened by success or failure in the workplace.' Jenny Groenewald, creative director at Hunt Lascaris FMC, puts it beautifully when she says, 'The main difference between men and women is that women don't feel the need to piss against every tree.'

If Japan and America have earthquakes, South Africa has socioquakes

The dramatic economic, social and political transformation of South Africa
has led to a socioquake registering 11 on the Richter scale. Our entire social
landscape has been rearranged by one socioquake after another, placing us all
under the most brutal pressure. Despite this, the root cause of burnout is not
external, it is inside us. Burnout is an abnormal response to an abnormal situation and that, believe it or not, is normal. So, if you are suffering from
burnout, know that you are normal. When people are confronted with a
bizarre present and an even stranger future, burnout is the sign of their
momentary loss of purpose and inner direction. Burnout is when we are
flooded with emotions that we cannot manage. Burnout is when we lose sight
of where we are headed or how we are going to get there.

We shall discuss the power of purpose and vision in the next chapter. Let
us now look at how we can all become masters of our emotions by control-
ling the fear that takes us into burnout. Being a controller of your fear means
never having to experience burnout again. Interested? Read on.

In this chaotic, turbulent, bonkers, frenzied, frightening, fast-forward environment, you had better be scared

Over the past year, we have worked with more than 200 companies throughout South Africa. In his self-appointed role as 'motivator to the nation', Mike
has personally spoken to more than 100 000 people. We have seen that the pace
of change, the violence, the uncertainty, the increased competition, the collapse of the rand, the corruption, the friction between government, business
and labour, the changing of the rules, the ongoing corporate downsizing, the
see-saw between black aspirations and white paranoia, have all contributed to
a national plague of fear and fatigue.

After a honeymoon that lasted about 18 months, reality has hit. The party
is over. Euphoria has been replaced with anxiety. It's hangover time. South
Africa's status as the darling of the world community has evaporated. The global spotlight has switched to another hot spot. We've had our 15 minutes of
fame. Now, we are just another emerging nation fumbling our way into the
future with ten steps forward, nine and a half steps back (yes, we do think South
Africa is inching forward). Clem Sunter expressed it best in the title of his
recent book, *Pretoria Will Provide and Other Myths*.

In this chaotic, turbulent, bonkers, frenzied, frightening, fast-forward
environment, you had better be scared. If you don't feel fear in the face of such
mayhem, you're probably lacking a chromosome or two. So relax. The real

point is not whether you feel the fear or not, it is what you do with it. We meet and counsel so many people who are hamstrung by their fears. They come to us for advice and when we give it to them they respond with the fatal words, 'Yes, but…', or 'What happens if I fail?'

The fact is that South Africa is not for the fainthearted. We have the highest rate of stressflation in the world — and it's only going to get higher. Jackie Mason, the well-known New York comedian, came to South Africa a few years ago and said, 'I dunno why you South Africans are so miserable. Heck, it's easy to be successful in South Africa. Hey, if you get through the day here, you're successful!' So, if you are looking outside yourself for solutions, you are looking in the wrong direction. Go within. Use your fear. Either you take the bull by the horns, or the bull takes you.

If you think the grass is greener on the other side, think again. We have both worked all over the world. The grass is not greener on the other side, it's just colder. If you think emigration is the way out, forget it. Fear is the global phenomenon of the nanosecond Nineties. Furthermore, the sense of alienation that many emigrants feel is profound. Mike knows. He was almost destroyed by it. Emigrants suffer from an extremely high incidence of strokes, cardiac arrests, cancers and psychological disorders such as acute depression. Speak to the wave of returning emigrants. At least you can wrestle with the devil you know.

What really turns us on about South Africa, though, is the possibilities of a country in transition. Neither of us could have achieved what we have achieved here anywhere else in the world. Says Reg, 'It is the powerful vibrancy and energy of South Africa that inspires the world-class work produced by leading South African advertising agencies. Since 1993, when South Africa was readmitted on to the world stage, two South African agencies were voted as being the best in the world by *Advertising Age*, the world's foremost advertising publication. Hunt Lascaris TBWA won the accolade in 1993 and Ogilvy & Mather in 1995. This is a truly remarkable achievement that reflects the power of harnessing this country's energy.'

Says Mike, 'For me, the irony is that I panicked and yielded to my own terror in one of the most stable, calmest cities in the world. *Time* magazine even called Toronto "New York run by the Swiss". I came back to South Africa to regain my sanity. It is this country that has given me back my life, my family, my *joie de vivre* and my purpose. So what I have learnt is that I take me wherever I go. Any which way I turn, my ass is always behind me.'

Jeremy Friedlander, partner in the highly successful property development company McCreedy Friedlander, expressed the possibilities offered by the new South Africa beautifully when he said to us: 'I know I could make it anywhere in the world. But I know I could not make it to the same degree that I am making it in South Africa. There is an explosion of so many opportunities in such a short space of time with so few people going for those opportunities. When I tell my counterparts overseas what I am doing here, they are stunned.'

Inspiration comes from the most unlikely sources. Recently, we were having a conversation with an Italian friend of ours. He told us that Italy has had one of the fastest-growing economies in Europe over the past 30 years. And yet they have also had a different government every 11 months. Their government is always in chaos and corruption. But the point our Italian friend made was that when the government is paralysed, the people continue about their lives unencumbered. We looked at each other and then told our friend that South Africa was heading along the same path as Italy with one major difference: in Italy, you first get into government, *then* you go to jail.

South Africa is the only country in the world that runs on miracles

Where were you on the morning of 10 April 1993? Do you even remember what happened that morning? It was an event that could have plunged South Africa into civil war: the assassination of Chris Hani, leader of the South African Communist Party. Do you remember how you felt when you heard that Hani had been murdered by a white man? What did you think was going to happen next? If you were like most South Africans, you probably thought that South Africa was going to become Bosnia Part Two.

What would you have said if we had told you on 10 April that South Africa would become the world's youngest democracy just a year later? What would you have said if we had told you that exactly 13 months later, 161 heads of state and senior government figures from around the world would gather together in Pretoria to celebrate Nelson Mandela's inauguration as the head of the rainbow nation? What would you have said if we had told you that Boutros Boutros-Ghali, Secretary General of the United Nations, would come to South Africa to attend the United Nations Conference on Trade and Industry and publicly say that South Africa is 'a light unto the nations'? We can tell you what you would have said: 'What are you smoking?'

This country has achieved the impossible and it continues to do so. Look at how far we have come since 1993 — and the journey has just begun. So what are the lessons that this country has taught us so far? We believe they can be summarised in three key action points:

See things the way they are. Don't be a Pollyanna pretending to yourself that everything is just hunky-dory. Take stock of both the positive and negative attributes of your specific situation in this country.

See things the way they can be. As we will share with you in the next chapter, don't forecast, backcast. Work back from the future. Look beyond the moment to what can be.

Make things the way they can be. Take action. Realise that you have the power to make a difference, because if not you, then who?

By the way, don't you think it is more than just coincidence that the leadership qualities of the two great figures of the twentieth century, Gandhi and Mandela, were forged in the heat of the South African experience?

Don't be a 'maybe' kind of person

The favourite emigration destinations of disgruntled South Africans are Canada, America, Britain and Australia. All of those countries have mature democracies and economies where almost everything has been done before. They have an established game, established rules and established players. At best, they are attempting reformation at the margin. In South Africa, we are boldly going where no one has ever gone before. We are attempting the total transformation of our society at warpspeed. We have no precedents to follow, only failures to avoid. Living in this country is like playing chess at 200 kilometres per hour.

If you can't deal with such fluidity, if you crave stability, order and predictability, you have a choice: either leave or learn not just to accept, but to love, stormy weather. But whatever you do, make the commitment. Don't run away from anything. Whenever you flee a situation because you believe you cannot handle it, you commit suicide by instalment. If you are going to leave, make sure that you are running to something that excites you. Whatever you do, don't sit on the fence, because it will only castrate you. Don't be a 'maybe' kind of person living a half life. 'Maybe' leads to 'If only', 'Why didn't I', 'I should have' — and life is too short and precious for that.

The bottom line is that South Africa in the last 1 000 days of the twentieth century has become a free-for-all — everything is up for grabs

South Africa will always be a polarised society. However, the new polarity is not between black and white: now there are just 264 shades of grey. The new polarity is between the magic and the tragic. It is no coincidence that South Africa has the highest rate of both miracles and murders per capita in the civilised world. The white waters of our society bring out either the best or the worst in people. What does South Africa bring out in you? The best or the worst you can be? Every time you blame what is going on around you for what is going on inside you, you abdicate your personal power.

The bottom line is that South Africa in the last 1 000 days of the twentieth century has become a free-for-all. Everything is up for grabs. When Thabo Mbeki publicly and proudly announces that he is a 'Thatcherite', one knows that the government has embraced capitalism with a vengeance — albeit capitalism with a conscience. The lesson here is that doing business in South Africa is a no-holds-barred contest. On the face of it, there are rules. But beneath the surface there is only one rule that counts: do whatever it takes, whenever you can, wherever it takes place. But do it with integrity, because the moment you lose integrity, you lose yourself. You have to be your own truth commission.

In medieval times, an alchemist was someone who could turn base metals into gold. In South Africa in the late 1990s, an alchemist is someone who can turn their fear into positive energy; who can turn the bad fear into the good fear. We believe that the good fear is the fuel of champions. The good fear sharpens the senses; it makes us more alert; it gets our heart pumping and our blood flowing; it opens the adrenalin valves; it readies us for action. The bad fear, on the other hand, is the panic, pessimism, personal helplessness, despair and depression that emotionally disembowel us. Have you noticed how many times you have been crippled by the bad fear when there was nothing to fear? How many times have you refrained from taking action because you were scared — only to look back at the situation moments later wondering why you were so scared, why you conjured up all the phantom consequences that would have resulted from taking action? You see, the bad fear really stands for False Evidence Appearing Real.

Stoke the fire of your 'good' fear

How you manage your fear is probably the biggest single factor that contributes to your personal success or failure. Are you even differentiating between the good fear and the bad fear? Or do you instinctively attempt to avoid any situation that makes you uncomfortable? We believe that you should only be uncomfortable when you are comfortable. There is no such thing as a comfort zone, only a stagnation zone. So we actively cultivate our fear, we stoke its fires, we work very hard at keeping our fears close to our heart so that we never lose our edge. Do you want to hear something astonishing? The best-performing athletes in the world are the athletes who are most scared before their race or contest. Those athletes who are completely relaxed before their event do not perform as well, because they do not use their fear to energise them effectively. The challenge is to love your fear, to embrace it, to celebrate it and let it turbocharge you. We'd like to share our fears with you:

Reg: 'I don't think I'll ever let go of the feeling that I can always do better. That's why I keep pushing myself. Despite what we write in this book, I am still scared of failure (although I'm working on it). In fact, the stakes are now higher than they have ever been. People are constantly expecting me to do something extraordinary. The higher I keep raising the bar, the higher I have to keep jumping. And that scares me. Whatever wealth I have achieved, I know it can be taken away in a heartbeat. I am scared of losing clients. I am scared of losing people close to me. I am scared that the competition is going to catch up with us. I am almost 50 and I am scared of going stale. Advertising is a young business and somehow I have to grow younger, not older. I'm scared of becoming irrelevant or losing my personal edge.'

Mike: 'Every time that I stand up to talk, I'm scared I'm going to stutter. And I'm scared of the embarrassment I feel when that happens. I'm scared before every talk that this time I won't connect with my audience, that I won't make them laugh or smile or cry. I'm scared that something will burst my dream. I feel that my life is too good to be true. I am scared that I am going to go out of fashion, that I will become yesterday's person. I'm scared that I won't be able to sustain my constant excitement and continual enthusiasm. Every month, I am scared that next month I won't get any assignments. Every day that I don't speak, I'm scared that it's the beginning of the end.'

If you permit your fears to lie like crocodiles in the murky pools of your subconscious, they will devour you

We believe that the moment you identify your fears, the moment you can stare at them, define them and give them perspective, is the moment that they lose their destructive power over you. It is when you permit them to lie like crocodiles in the murky pools of your subconscious that they devour you. They're deep, they're dark, they're going to get you. You cannot confront what you cannot see. And it is what you cannot see that scares you shitless. So we hope you spent some time answering the questions at the beginning of this chapter. All the emotions outlined in the last question are fear's closest relatives. And unless you are Roboperson, you have probably experienced most — if not all — of those emotions during the past three months. Our point here, though, is firstly the need to recognise the emotion when you are experiencing it, and then to ask yourself what the signal is that the emotion is sending you. This endeavour takes two vital qualities:

☛ It takes courage. We're asking you to become a psychonaut, to venture into your own mind and to explore what you may have been afraid to explore until now. Remember, courage is not the absence of fear, it is the determination to act in the face of it. It is the defining characteristic of every truly effective person we have met. Truly effective people do things that other people shy away from because they are afraid or unwilling to do them.

☛ It takes self-awareness, the ability to step outside of yourself and to observe your emotions and actions. Most of us live our lives unconsciously. We feel things and we do things without even being aware of what we are feeling or doing. From this moment on, switch off your automatic pilot and concentrate on understanding yourself. Again, this takes practice. Make self-awareness a habit. Start right now. What are you feeling as you read this passage, and why are you feeling it? Is it an empowering emotion or a disempowering one? What do you need to do either to sustain your positive emotions or to transform your negative ones?

Let's look at some of the signals that fear and its associated emotions send us:

Fear: South Africa is a country driven by fear. The national media feeds off it. Every day we read, see and hear stories of horror, savagery, crime and catastrophe. It is easy to become addicted to it, because we get a perverse charge from fear. It is also easy to give in to the fear, to let it dominate our thinking and control our behaviour. *Caveat,* South Africans.

The real message of fear, though, is simply that something is about to happen that we need to prepare for. When we underestimate our ability to handle what is about to happen, fear turns into panic, worry or anxiety. Think about the huge challenges that you have overcome in your life. Think about the acts of courage and the sheer guts that got you to where you are now. Now think about whether the outside event that is causing you such concern really justifies it.

When we are in a crisis, we very often suffer from instant amnesia. We forget what we are capable of doing. We are hijacked by our fear. From this moment on, we ask you to evaluate your current challenge in the context of what you have already achieved. You will discover that there is very little that you cannot handle. Remember the universal truth: God does not give us anything that we cannot handle.

Show no fear: Whether you do feel the fear or not, do not show it. No matter what the situation, master your fear on the outside. Like all other mammals, humans can immediately sense when somebody is in the grip of fear. Think about your own personal circumstance: what happens to your willingness to follow or to listen to another person when you perceive them to be scared or uncertain? Even muggers will go for the person they sense is apprehensive or fearful. That is why we have to work at harnessing our fear so that it serves us and does not debilitate us.

Every day of our lives, the two of us do things that we are not quite sure of. We are always operating at the edge of our competence with one foot in the unknown. If we ever allowed the people we work with to get the sense that we are frightened, our leverage and credibility would be severely diminished. What can we say, except that life is a game of poker? (And if you are playing a game of poker and you can't find the sucker, leave. You're the sucker.)

Hurt: The message of hurt is simply that we have allowed somebody else to control our emotions. We have allowed somebody else's actions or words to pull us down. We often ascribe to people motives that they do not have. If someone close to you doesn't keep a commitment to you or they talk to you in a way that you believe is demeaning, it may not have anything to do with you; it may have everything to do with them, with a crisis that they are trying to manage. But how often do you immediately come to the conclusion that their express purpose through this action or omission was to hurt you?

Remember: no one can hurt you unless you give them permission to do so.

Anger: This is the emotion that people find most difficult to control. The message of anger is that an important rule of yours has been violated or that your emotions are in disequilibrium. It is not the snake bite that kills you, it is the spread of poison. It is not what people say or do to you, it is how you interpret what they have done or said to you. The next time you feel yourself getting angry, ask yourself whether the person even knows what they have done, or whether they are just the trigger for your internal explosion.

Remember: every time that you attack others, you wound yourself. Anger cannibalises your energy. No one can think clearly with clenched fists.

Anger does more damage to relationships than any other emotion. How many times has someone said something to you in anger that cut you deeply? Don't you always think of what they said to you whenever you see this person? Sticks and stones can break your bones, but words screw you up for life! When people say they've buried the hatchet, they never forget where. So, before you get angry, consider three things:

☞ Does this person really mean to hurt me? If the answer's no, don't become angry.
☞ Does this person really care for me? If the answer's yes, don't become angry.
☞ Is this person struggling with their own personal pain? If the answer's yes, don't become angry.

One night, while he was hosting Power Talk, a caller named Deidre phoned in to tell Mike he was a fake. She sounded furious as she accused him of not acknowledging the sources of his information. Mike responded by saying that the listeners to the programme didn't care where the ideas came from, they just wanted to hear the message. Finally, in jest, Mike advised Deidre not to be so cynical. Deidre responded by shouting into the phone, 'I'm not cynical, asshole!!' Mike resisted the urge to become angry by asking: Did Deidre really mean to hurt him? Answer: no. Was she struggling with her own anger? Answer: yes. Therefore Mike didn't become angry.

Every action that another human being takes towards you is either a loving response or it is a cry for help. When people engage in acts of affection or kindness, they are demonstrating their caring for others. But when they lose their temper, they are really demonstrating their inability to manage their own emotions. Deidre insulted Mike because she could not engage in verbal sparring with him, and so she retreated to her last resort: anger.

We can almost hear what you're thinking: it is easier said than done. We agree. Resisting anger takes practice. So start practising today. Reg comments, 'I am bombarded by problems every day. The advertising business is only about people. And so 99 per cent of those problems are related to people. Many of them are caused by insensitivity, negligence, ego, personality clashes, rejection or plain paranoia. If I allowed myself to become angry, I wouldn't be able to handle my job. So I work very hard not to lose my temper. I've come to the point where I'm pretty good at staying calm. But when I do become angry, I erupt like a volcano. Fortunately, that happens very seldom. And it is almost always when someone sets out deliberately to harm either me or the agency.'

Frustration: The message of frustration is an exciting one. It is that you are on a growth path. Frustration tells you that you feel you could be doing better but have not yet discovered a way of doing so. It tells you that you are about to have a breakthrough. Use the emotion of frustration to energise yourself. When you get down on yourself, you minimise your effectiveness and heighten your personal discomfort. Remember: frustration is foreplay to achievement.

The challenge of frustration is to channel its energy. Frustration is like the dam wall that blocks the river's flow. Hydro-electricity is produced by the programmed release of the water's flow. Know then, that your frustration is really the building-up of energy that is about to produce your personal power.

Disappointment: The message offered by disappointment is that you have an expectation that is not going to be met. Disappointment is your signal to evaluate your expectations for their validity, to change them so that they are more appropriate to the situation, and then to take action to fulfil your revised expectations. Remember that God's delays are not God's denials. How many times have you been disappointed — only to find that what happened subsequently surpassed your original expectations?

Mike talks from experience when he says, 'One of the reasons why I became so depressed is that I saw my dream of running a massive advertising agency slipping away from me. The more I realised that my expectations were not going to be met, the more demoralised I became. However, when I look at what I am doing now, when I see the faces of all the thousands of people I motivate every month, I know that I am far better suited to my current calling than I ever would have been as the head of an advertising agency.'

If there is one key characteristic of great achievers, it is their ability to manage disappointment. When we feel disappointed, many of us give up. We resign ourselves to the fact that our desires will not be met. However, success is primarily a result of hanging on when everybody else has let go. As Winston Churchill said, 'Never, never, never give up.'

Guilt: Guilt is a killer. The message of guilt is that you may be allowing other people's expectations of you to dictate your life. There are so many people who live a life of misery because they feel a false sense of obligation to other people's hopes and wishes. Time and time again, we hear people say to us, 'I can't let so-and-so down.' Many people sacrifice their own well-being for the acceptance of themselves by others. The emotion of guilt is your signal to take charge of your own destiny. Don't·let someone else's prejudices become your burden.

Suzette van der Merwe, the stunning ex-Miss South Africa and now a highly successful entrepreneur who manages the careers of a number of celebrities, tells how she fought and won her battle against guilt: 'I come from a very conservative background. I became Miss South Africa at the age of 21. In just one year, I appeared on 105 magazine covers. I got married at 22. I was seen to have it all. I became a kind of icon for Afrikaans women. But I became weary of my life as a public figure and it became clear to me that my marriage wasn't working. However, because of my background which frowned on divorce, and the expectations of thousands of people who viewed me as their role model living the perfect life, I continued to live my life according to my public image. However, my unhappiness eventually reached such a point that I decided to take action. I got divorced and reduced my public profile. It wasn't easy, but now, for the first time, I'm living my life according to what's good for me. I'm not sure what the future holds for me yet. At the moment, I'm just going with the flow. But I've never been happier. I am free.'

Inadequacy: The signal of inadequacy is that you may not have sufficient skills or confidence for the challenge at hand. Don't allow inadequacy to paralyse you. Establish whether you need to acquire more skills or whether you just need to acquire more confidence. In both cases, you have the power to do whatever it takes to rise to the challenge. The greatest human tragedy is the tragedy that plays itself out in thousands of situations in South Africa every day: people who jail themselves in their own mental prisons because of their feelings of inadequacy. So make a decision: either you want to live half a life, or you want to fly. The choice is yours. Exorcise the feeling of inadequacy from your emotional repertoire. And know this: no one really knows what is going on in this country any more. No matter how educated or experienced people may be, we are all just dancing in the dark.

Confusion: People feel confused whenever their beliefs are shown to be no longer valid, and when they have not yet formed new beliefs appropriate to changed circumstances. Confusion is a positive signal: it means that you are going through the process of transformation. If you are not confused by what is currently happening in South Africa, you are probably totally out of touch with your environment. Remember the force of flow. If you don't flow, you don't grow. Be prepared to be surprised, be prepared to change. The river that runs to the sea is constantly changing form and swirling round obstacles — but it never changes direction.

Johnny Clegg, one of the world's most successful musicians, expresses his thoughts on confusion: 'I think all the views we have on the world come originally from our backgrounds — family, state, church, school, etc. A lot of us stay prisoners of those views our whole lives. But some of us manage to throw off those things or shed those values that do not serve us any longer. But this shedding process can be incredibly painful. It means having to reinvent yourself and re-examining all you have been told.'

Feeling overwhelmed: The fear that we will not be able to cope with all the pressures and challenges confronting us is a huge fear that is disempowering South Africans. The message that this emotion is sending us is to *chunk down*. By this we mean to prioritise what needs to be done and then to focus on just one thing, one day at a time. How many times have you been in a meeting with someone while you were thinking about what you forgot to do elsewhere, or what you still had to do, or what was going to happen the following day? *Carpe diem*, seize the moment, seize the day. Focus on doing well what you are doing at that particular moment, and the future will take care of itself.

At a talk we delivered together, we were approached by a woman who is a member of Alcoholics Anonymous (AA). She was so moved by our talk that she gave us a little card containing the AA creed. We were so impressed with the basic wisdom contained in the card that we have reproduced a portion of it for you here:

☞ **Just for today** I will try to live through this day only, and not tackle my whole life problem at once.

☞ **Just for today** I will be happy.

☞ **Just for today** I will adjust myself to what is, and not try to adjust everything to my own desires.

☞ **Just for today** I will try to strengthen my mind. I will study. I will learn something useful.

☞ **Just for today** I will be agreeable. I will look as well as I can, dress becomingly, act courteously, criticise not one bit, not find fault with anything, and not try to improve or regulate anybody except myself.

☛ **Just for today** I will have a programme. I may not follow it exactly but I will have it. I will save myself from two pests: hurry and indecision.

☛ **Just for today** I will have a quiet half-hour all by myself, and relax. During this half-hour, some time, I will try to get a better perspective of my life.

☛ **Just for today** I will be unafraid. Especially I will not be afraid to enjoy what is beautiful, and to believe that as I give to the world, so the world will give to me.

Burnout: As we have seen, burnout is when you have allowed the feeling of being overwhelmed to consume you entirely. Burnout is when you feel hopeless, because your current strategy of managing life is ineffective. The message burnout is sending you is to put some distance between yourself and the problems that you cannot manage, even if it is for a short period of time. After this, you need to redesign both your life and the way you are managing it.

Failure: In all the workshops that we have conducted with thousands of South Africans over the past year, by far the single biggest fear expressed by people is the fear of failure. But what is the fear of failure? It is simply the fear of not achieving our goals or targets. We are afraid that if we do not meet these goals we will lose faith in ourselves and we will lose face with others. This fear is so great that many of us perform well below our potential. Rather than stretch ourselves and suffer the self-inflicted humiliation of possible defeat, we don't place ourselves at risk — for fear of failure.

What is the message that fear of failure is sending you? It is telling you to change your rules regarding failure. Our definition of failure is when we don't try something new. We know that every experience in the pursuit of growth is a learning experience that will benefit us in the long run. Ben Cohen, who founded a chain of ice cream stores in the USA called Ben & Jerry's, expressed the perfect way to regard failure. He said, 'I would rather fail at something new, than succeed at what I already know how to do.'

Fear of failure is what prevents so many people from trying something new. The pain and threat associated with being seen to stumble overpowers the potential pleasure derived from mastering a new skill or embarking on a new venture. The emotional risk is simply too high. Champion South Africans, on the other hand, know that not to try is to fail. What's more, they actually celebrate failures.

Arthur Gillis, managing director of the highly successful Protea Hospitality Group, and his team of directors have actually initiated an annual award for the most spectacular screw-ups committed by Protea Hotels employees during the year. They call it the Golden Lemon Award. At their annual management award ceremonies, the Golden Lemon Award is positioned as the main award of the evening. Inevitably, the winners of this dubious accolade are the senior management of the chain. This is how the award is described in a public announcement: 'This award goes to the Head Office person who has made the biggest contribution towards providing this organisation with outrageous stupidity.' In the past two years, the award has gone to the chairman of the company and the financial director. Gillis says that the objective of the award is to remove the fear of failure from his organisation, and to demonstrate that no matter how smart or how senior someone is, they will always make mistakes.

Raymond Ackerman put it nicely when he said, 'People who don't make mistakes, usually don't make anything.' And we like Stan Katz's quote when he said, 'Go out there and make mistakes, but for God's sake, make new mistakes!'

The only time that you truly fail is when you quit: that is when your spirit dies and with it the potential to grow. Vince Lombardi, the legendary coach of the American football team the Greenbay Packers, expressed his disbelief in failure when he retired from coaching after a career that spanned 30 years. 'In all my years of coaching,' he said, 'I never lost a game. Sometimes, I just ran out of time.' Isn't that magnificent?

Success: The fear of success is almost as great as the fear of failure. We all have an internal emotional barometer. We perform best at a certain emotional temperature. Physically, our bodies perform efficiently at 36,8 degrees Celsius. When it drops below that temperature, the body will heat itself. When it rises above that temperature, it will cool itself. The same applies to our minds. The challenge that we all face is to raise the mental and emotional temperature that we are comfortable with.

Think about when you have done extremely well. Think about the jump in other people's expectations of you. Think about the increased pressure to perform. Think about the increased stress that comes from having to consistently meet the higher standards you have set for yourself. Think about how much more you have to lose when you ascend the ladder of success. Scary, isn't it? So:

☛ Don't look down; look up. Don't contemplate what happens if you fall. Because if you focus on your fear, it will get you.

☛ Understand that no matter how well you've done, you've barely begun to unleash your potential.

☛ There is no such thing as failure; only learning experiences.

☛ Measure yourself against yourself, not against others. Don't try to be better than anybody else, strive to be the best that you can be!

Pessimism: The most superb definition of pessimism comes from Webster's Dictionary: it is 'the tendency to see or anticipate only what is disadvantageous or futile in current or future conditions or actions, often when it is reasonably possible to see or anticipate advantage or gains'. So when you are feeling pessimistic, re-evaluate your perceptions of future events and pinpoint the promise that your current mindset may be overlooking.

But how do you really know whether you are a pessimist or not? Here is a quick ten-point checklist from an article on optimism in the August 1996 issue of *Cosmopolitan* magazine written by Nadine Rubin and based largely on Mike's input and that of Dorianne Weil, 702 Talk Radio's Dr D:

Pessimists versus optimists

☛ A pessimist asks, 'Why me?'
An optimist feels empowered to deal with situations.

☛ Pessimists are convinced that if something bad happens once, it's going to recur.
Optimists generalise less. They see unpleasant incidents as separate from future predictability.

☛ A pessimist sees a problem as a sign that their life is a mess.
An optimist never sees a problem as permanent.

☛ A pessimist makes one mistake at work and thinks she's going to be fired.
An optimist realistically evaluates the reasons behind her mistakes.

☛ A pessimist has a fight with her lover and decides he doesn't love her.
An optimist sees the fight as a moment of disagreement that will pass.

☛ When a pessimist does something well, she thinks anyone could have done it.
An optimist feels pride at others' praise.

☞ A pessimist is certain that two people whispering are talking about her.
An optimist is sure that they're speaking quietly among themselves.

☞ A pessimist forgets her brother's birthday and thinks she's a bad person.
An optimist apologises and makes it up to him.

☞ A pessimist pigs out on chocolate and immediately feels guilty.
An optimist sees it as a temporary diet lapse.

☞ When the value of the rand goes down and the price of petrol goes up, a pessimist says, 'I should've known to leave this country before the rand dropped so low. How could I have been so stupid?'
An optimist says, 'I must plan my finances carefully so that I make the most of the money I do have.'

So how did you score? If you identified with the response of the pessimist more than three times, you have some major attitude adjusting to do.

So what is the antidote to pessimism and fear? What is the beacon that guides us through the darkness?

Three

Faith: The ultimate resource

What was it that sustained Nelson Mandela for 27 years while he sat in his prison cell? What was it that empowered Victor Frankl to survive for four years in the hell called Auschwitz? What was it that encouraged Christopher Columbus to embark on his voyage of discovery? What was it that strengthened FW de Klerk to willingly hand over the reigns of power despite enormous resistance from within his party? What is it that motivates any champion to brave the terrors of the unknown? What is it that inspires people to do things they are not sure they can do? What is the ultimate attribute of the thousands of entrepreneurs who put their life on the line every year to live their dream? The one-word answer: faith.

Faith is a powerful belief in something, even when you do not have any external proof of its existence. It is an emphatic conviction that carries you through all fears, uncertainties and doubts. Faith is, quite simply, the ultimate resource. It is, without exception, the hallmark of human greatness. Without it, you will always be a follower walking in someone else's footsteps. Do you have faith? Are you searching for faith? Are you channelling its power effectively? Take a moment to consider the following Seven Questions of Faith that will become your personal blueprint for fulfilment and success. Don't worry if you can't answer these questions straight away — it could take you the next few months to recognise what fuels your faith. The important issue here is that you start the process of deciding your path that leads you to your destiny. This chapter is our attempt to inspire and coach you through the process.

Seven questions of faith

Purpose

Are you living your life according to a purpose? What is your purpose? What is the primary benefit that you deliver to life and other people?

. . . .
. . . .
. . . .
. . . .

Identity

Who are you really? How do you define yourself? What is your personal identity? Why are you unique?

. . . .
. . . .

. . . .
. . . .

Core beliefs

What are your core empowering beliefs? What kind of feelings of certainty do you have that make you a tough-minded optimist?

. . . .
. . . .
. . . .
. . . .

Values

What are your values? What are your personal principles that guide your interaction with other people and your decisions?

. . . .
. . . .
. . . .
. . . .
. . . .

Behaviour

How do you express your purpose, identity, values and beliefs through your behaviour? How do you conduct yourself towards other people? What do you do daily to maximise your influence and personal power towards others?

. . . .
. . . .
. . . .
. . . .
. . . .

Strategic plan

What is your personal strategic plan to achieve your purpose? What actions do you need to take consistently to become everything you know you can be?

. . . .
. . . .
. . . .
. . . .
. . . .

One-year goals

What are your top five measurable one-year goals that you have set for yourself to achieve your purpose?

☞ . . . .
. . . .
☞ . . . .
. . . .
☞ . . . .
. . . .
☞ . . . .
. . . .
☞ . . . .
. . . .

Once you have read through this chapter, copy these Seven Questions of Faith and think them through whenever you have a quiet moment.

Before you can make a great dream come true, you need a great dream

'Get your motor running
Get out on the highway
Looking for adventure
In whatever comes my way'

— STEPPENWOLF, 'Born to be Wild'

When it comes to demonstrating the power of faith, nothing illustrates it better than the following stories of the extraordinary South Africans who understand one inspiring truth: if you can dream it, you can do it. The moment you commit yourself to greatness with such an intensity that you eliminate all your doubts, then the higher power works with you to make it happen. But before you can make a great dream come true, you need to have a great dream. And you need to take the first step.

Prepare to be inspired

First, a lovely little joke on taking action. Abe Cohen is a very observant Jew who attends synagogue every Sabbath. He is also a highly compassionate, generous man who does unto others as he would have them do unto him. But Abe has become increasingly angry with his Creator, and one Friday night in the synagogue, he looks skyward and whispers, 'You know, God, it's not fair. Here I sit, as I do every Sabbath, observing my faith. I do only good towards my fellow human beings of all creeds, classes and colours. And yet I look around me and see all my friends winning the lottery. Some of them are not even nice people. They cheat, they lie, they commit adultery, they don't even know what the inside of a house of God looks like. But, despite my good deeds, I win nothing. I'm telling you, God, it's not fair.' All of a sudden, Abe hears a thunderous voice in his head, 'Abe, meet me halfway! Buy a ticket!' Well, have you bought your ticket yet? Let's look at some people who have!

How Khethla Mthembu met his destiny halfway

Khethla Mthembu is the head of New Age Beverages, the company that manufactures and markets Pepsi in South Africa. He told Mike on Power Talk how he met his destiny halfway. 'I have always been a restless person. I was always looking for bigger and better challenges. I went into the insurance business in the early eighties, but I soon tired of working for somebody else. I knew I was not meant to be an employee. So I started my own insurance company. I remember that when I told my dad that I was going into business for myself, he thought I was going to buy someone's shop. He said, "That's great, we never have to buy groceries again," because he automatically assumed that every black person who ran a business was the owner of either a store or a taxi. Anyway, I started my business in 1983 and built it into AFGEN, one of the largest short-term insurance companies in South Africa and the first black-controlled insurance company.

'After Nelson Mandela was released, it became very clear to my colleagues and me that this country was going through a change that no one could stop. It was also clear that many companies which had disinvested because of apartheid would return. I went abroad and spoke to many of these companies. One of these companies was Pepsi. Pepsi was the company that was most ready to return. I looked at the cola market and the battle that would follow and decided that my whole restlessness would be well accommodated by the challenges offered in this venture. What we did was to challenge those people who used to lead marches and protests against apartheid. We went to them and thanked them for their support in the past. But we said now was the time for them to help rebuild South Africa by investing in it. It is incredibly satisfying and exciting when I think of their response. The array of investors in

Pepsi's return to South Africa include Danny Glover, Whitney Houston, Johnny Cochran, and Shaquille O'Neal, amongst others.

'We realise that we have a very formidable competitor in Coca-Cola. They have enjoyed a monopoly for about 15 years. But I have always loved competition. Every time I think about the challenge ahead of us, I get goosebumps. You see, I have learnt to challenge what other people call insurmountable obstacles. This is my new struggle. I want to convert people to Pepsi now. No one expected that a black person would actually come into South Africa and challenge a giant like Coca-Cola. But we are doing it. I'm living my dream. Obviously part of my motivation is commercial, but it goes way beyond that. I am out to prove what black business people can really achieve. When I go into the townships, people say to me, "Gee, we can't believe that Pepsi is really your company." They still believe that a black person in business must be running a corner shop. So my mission is to continually change my people's orientation from a politically inclined mind to an economically inclined mind. Because true empowerment is economic empowerment.

'It's amazing that the Pepsi slogan — "The Choice of a New Generation" — was originated 17 years ago. That slogan is perfect for the new South Africa. When I see kids of all colours getting excited about Pepsi, I know that there is a new generation in South Africa. We are not a black choice. We are not a white choice. We are the choice of a new generation. And we are investing more than R400 million over a period of three years to make our vision a reality — and already our sales are greatly outstripping our expectations.'

How Herman Mashaba's faith beat the system

Herman Mashaba, founder and chief executive of the highly successful Black Like Me haircare products company, is a walking example of the power of faith. 'We are dealing in a market where we are competing with multinational companies with more money than we could ever dream of. So, although we are a big company from a South African perspective, from a global perspective we are very small. But at the end of the day we want to be big. A few years ago I took my team with me into the bush where we looked at our future. And I said to them, "Where do you guys believe we should be taking this company?" My management team and I decided that we were going to be a brand leader, not on a global level, but on the African continent. We know this continent better than any multinational in this business. Within the next ten years we will achieve our goal. We have the strategies and programmes in place to make it happen.

'But you know what? Despite our size and what we have achieved, I never, ever say to myself, "Herman, you're successful." I have a very vulnerable kind of business and although it may appear from the outside that I'm successful, I know that as long as I'm alive, I'll never rest. Because I know where I've come from and what it took to get me to where I am today. You see, I grew up in a township about 30 kilometres north of Pretoria. I looked at the black men around me and I saw people who had their pride stripped away from them. As I was growing up in the township, I remember my friends going into the white neighbourhoods to find work as "garden boys". I promised myself that I would never allow myself to be denigrated, exploited or humiliated as a person. I said to myself, "No way, I'm not prepared to subject myself to this. I'd rather stay in the township and find other means of making money." Because, if you subject yourself to that kind of indignity, you end up being defeated inside. And that's actually what has happened to many black people in this country. They have accepted humiliation as part of their lives. Before anything else, therefore, I believe the real challenge for the majority of South Africans is mental liberation from this mindset.

'I started my first formal job in 1980, and spent the next three years as somebody else's employee. I had just married and a few months later I bought a car. That's when I said to myself, "Herman Mashaba, this is the end of your career working for someone else." When I told my wife, she became angry with me because she thought we needed a guaranteed salary. I told her, "Look around you. Look at the township, look at my mother, look at your parents, look at everyone around us. Do you expect me to go through my life the same miserable way as all these people? No way, there must be a better way. Let me go out and try it on my own."

'The first thing I tried was insurance. During the first month I realised that I was in the wrong game. So I opened the paper and looked at the ads for sales reps. At one stage I was selling for four companies at the same time. But you know what infuriated me? While I was trying to make an honest living through tears and guts, I was made a criminal in my own country by the pass laws. I don't think white people have even the slightest idea what the pass laws really used to mean to us. You see, by being a self-employed black man, I was breaking the law. I was tormented by knowing that I could be thrown into jail at any time. It made me hate everything about this country. Although I'm a forward thinker, I am still angry at the people who were responsible for that injustice.

'Fortunately, I survived without ever being arrested, but millions of my people weren't so lucky. They were put in jail. And every time a guy is put in jail, he is placed with criminals. This means that when he comes out, he has a greater chance of becoming a criminal himself. So although apartheid is no more, I'll never forget what it did to me and my people. In a strange way, though, apartheid was responsible for me getting into haircare. Because of the pass laws, I used to monitor the police movements. And the only way I could monitor their movements was to know the area that I operated in very well. That obviously greatly restricted my mobility and my market. I was forced to keep returning to the same customers again and again. So, I was always on the lookout for new products to sell to my customers. But what I really wanted was the kind of product that required constant reordering and service. Unfortunately, I couldn't find such a product.

'One day I saw an ad recruiting salespeople for a haircare company in the newspaper. I phoned the company only to be told that they were looking for white salespeople. I nevertheless persuaded them to see me. I went for an interview and ten minutes later had the job, also on a commission basis, because I was not prepared to accept any job where somebody else decided my income. I wanted to sign my own cheque. And that's how I got into the cosmetics and haircare industry. I started my job the next morning and within a few hours I knew that this was what I had been looking for. First of all, it was a product I would use personally. And secondly, it meant that I could service the same people again and again in my territory.

'I worked for that company for almost two years. And I made a lot of money. But I began to dream of succeeding on my own. I started talking to black salon owners, and they promised me that they would support me if I could make my own quality product. And that's how Black Like Me was born. The salon owners were true to their word. They supported me. I didn't make it because I was clever. I made it because of my faith in other people who did not let me down.'

Mashaba's words echo the message of Leo Buscalia, one of America's leading motivationalists and the self-proclaimed 'professor of love'. Buscalia states that he would rather look for the good in everybody and trust people and be cheated once or twice, than live his whole life in fear and suspicion.

Dennis Mashabela's divine insanity

In a way, faith is really a form of divine insanity. Consider the story of Dennis Mashabela, founder and managing director of Mashabela Burrows, one of South Africa's exciting new advertising agencies with clients like Radio Metro, South African Airways, Pretoria Portland Cement and AT&T.

'I had got to the point where I felt strangled by the environment of the company I was working for. I didn't respect the intellect of the people with whom

I was working. I was not being fulfilled. I needed new challenges. I used to get up in the morning and not feel like going to the office. Every day that happened, a little part of me died. Now, I know a lot of people find themselves in this position, but most of them just winge, moan and complain. I came to the point where I decided not to spend a day longer doing what I wasn't happy doing, because you can't compromise on your happiness. That's one of my principles. But principles cost you money; in fact, it's not a principle until it costs you money.

'I decided to take a leap of faith. I resigned and started my own advertising agency with a partner, Paul Burrows. I gave up my equity in my previous company and we began our agency without a single client, which was madness, really, especially as I had just bought a house. But I have seen so many people fall into the trap of using their financial commitments as an excuse not to exercise their faith. My point of view was exactly the opposite: I couldn't afford not to take the risk, because you can't put a price on happiness. Because I have a bond and kids, I shall not falter. I am going to do extremely well or die trying. But you can imagine what my wife's response was when I told her we may not be able to pay the bond a couple of months from then.

'Our massive breakthrough came when Radio Metro put its account out for pitch. We managed to get on to the list of candidate agencies together with the big guns of the industry, including Hunt Lascaris TBWA, Saatchi & Saatchi and Partnership. It really was a case of David versus the Goliaths. They may have been "world class", but we were micro-class. And we won. I don't think I've ever got so smashed in my life. The win catapulted us into a new dimension. It allowed us to flex our creative muscles and show what we were really capable of doing. Since then, our business has grown exponentially and, yes, I did meet my mortgage payments.'

At the time of writing this book, Mashabela had just concluded a deal with Leo Burnett, one of the world's largest agencies. His little agency now has global clout. We have included Mashabela's story as a call to action to all those people who use the false justification of financial or family burdens to excuse themselves from pursuing their dream. Remember the definition of a coward: a hero with a spouse, kids and a mortgage.

How Johnny Clegg beats the block

No matter who you are or how switched on you are, there will always be those moments when your inspiration, hope, creativity, energy, joy or will to win momentarily deserts you. Johnny Clegg describes the bridging role that faith plays when he is in nowhereland.

'In almost every music-recording project, I hit a patch where I dry up. I just can't take myself to the next stage. I have learnt to be patient and wait for the inspiration to shine through once more. I have learnt not to despair, because my creativity will suddenly come through again. I think it's a kind of faith in the creative process. You have to have a fundamental trust that the inspiration will reappear. You know, if artists knew exactly where their creativity came from, there would be no such thing as writer's block or artist's block. I think inspiration comes from a very mysterious place, but you have to do all you can to reach this secret place.'

How Anant Singh defied all odds

Anant Singh is indisputably South Africa's leading film producer with such internationally acclaimed films as 'Cry, the Beloved Country' (with Richard Harris and James Earl Jones), 'Sarafina' (with Whoopi Goldberg) and 'A Place of Weeping' to his credit. He has also been charged with production of the film of Mandela's autobiography, *Long Walk to Freedom*. Professionally, he is a creature of apartheid who was oppressed by it and yet profited from outwitting it. We asked Singh what he believed was the most important contributor to his success. 'My faith in my intuition. When I feel that a particular concept has huge potential, I will go with it, despite the doubts and negative feedback of others. I have learnt to have faith in my judgement and not to be infected by the scepticism of others.'

The story on Anant Singh that follows was drawn from conversations that Mike had with him, as well as reports in the *New York Times* and *Ebony South Africa* magazine.

To make a good film, you need time to prepare. In Hollywood, there are too many people trying to make 300-odd films a year. The industry there is committee-driven, from scriptwriting down to cutting, and in the end, they have to rush things, which makes things more expensive. If you need two production people, a studio in Hollywood wants 20 because no one wants to make a decision. Then the costs — hotels, catering — compound. Singh chooses to stay in South Africa where he can produce a film for half the price it would cost in Hollywood. He travels to America every four to six weeks to keep a finger on the pulse of the movie capital, but remains independent enough to 'reflect on priorities'.

It is this shrewd instinct that has driven Singh to the heights he has reached after 21 years in the film industry. He started as a film winder in a small business renting out 16 mm films before the days of video. His starting salary was R1 a day. But, says Singh, 'I got to see the movies and I got to take the movies home. When I told my mother that I wanted to work in films, she thought I was totally out of my mind. She tried to get everyone to talk me out of it.'

Instead of complying, he followed two paths — studying for a degree in engineering while working for the film rental company. In the end it paid off. When the owner of the rental company offered to sell it to Singh, he jumped at the opportunity. He bought the company but kept it registered in the owner's name: he was forbidden by law to own a business in the centre of Durban because he was 'non-white'.

The rental business prospered with the advent of videos, and soon he began distributing films to cinemas. Astutely, he started buying the South African rights to foreign films, haggling Hollywood studio demands down from $20 000 to $1 000 or so. His first big success was 'Secrets', a forgettable film resurrected only because it featured Jacqueline Bisset minus the wet T-shirt she had just made famous in 'The Deep'.

Under South Africa's bizarre censorship laws of the time, Singh was jailed for showing the James Bond film 'Live and Let Die' to friends. 'Yaphet Kotto (a black actor) slapped Jane Seymour around in it, so only whites were allowed to see it!' Singh explains. Many American films that his customers wanted to see were banned, like 'Guess Who's Coming to Dinner', which starred Sidney Poitier and showed blacks and whites socialising together. Singh sometimes appealed against the bannings. 'The board in Pretoria was six clearly rightwing guys,' he says. 'The minute I appeared, you could see their arrogance coming out.' At first Singh never won. Then, when he could afford to hire a white lawyer, he occasionally did win an appeal. Sometimes he flouted the law and simply bought the rights and showed the film. 'It was forbidden fruit,' he says, 'but it was the way we learned about another culture. For us, there was no other way to see films with black heroes.'

Later, he embarked on a career in production. 'At that time, the business was dominated by white males and the structure was set up to support Afrikaans films. I had to prove a point to myself and beat the odds stacked against me. It was a lot of hard work. On all levels I found resistance, including being arrested, and I had difficulties getting credit.'

Singh's first film was called 'A Place of Weeping'. It was about a brutal white farmer who fatally beats a worker who simply wanted enough to eat. It was made in 14 days and cost less than R100 000, a laughable price for a feature film. Singh had to fund the film himself, though. Not only would it have been difficult for a black man to get that kind of credit, but the subject of the film would have made it impossible. He quickly realised that if he was determined to do the film, he would have to go it alone. And so he invested almost everything he had in making it.

'When I was producing "A Place of Weeping", which was the first anti-apartheid film to be shown in South Africa, the police were constantly chasing and harassing us. We made this film on the run. Every day, the police would show up at the location where we'd been the day before. When we finished filming, I took the rolls of film under my arm and immediately flew with them to London.' The next day, the police arrived at his Durban office, demanding them. He arranged for the film's commercial opening in New York, correctly betting that the Pretoria censors wouldn't risk international humiliation by banning a political film at home that major American critics had praised.

Today, after the international acclaim and commercial success of 'Sarafina' and 'Cry, the Beloved Country', Singh has fewer problems getting financing for his films, although it is still not easy. 'With bigger projects it is harder to get investors, and you have to make a commitment yourself.' Singh is now 39 years old. He has produced 40 films. An unapologetic professional, he is very particular about the scripts he will look at. 'Everyone has a film idea, crazy though it may be,' he says. 'I don't accept unsolicited scripts; the person has to go through an agent first.' How does he choose which films to do? 'I have to be committed to it and it has to have a place in my heart or else I won't do it.'

Ebony South Africa magazine says that Singh's success has made him 'one of South Africa's primary culture gurus'. Despite his success, Singh remains humble. 'My sense of accomplishment is dealing with everything on a day-to-day basis. My philosophy is to take care of today and tomorrow will take care of itself. This is a very intensive and high-powered business. I tend to get on with doing what I have to do and don't worry about what the next person is doing.'

Singh's next project is perhaps the most coveted film script in the world: Nelson Mandela's autobiography. Singh is faced with condensing the 617 pages of *Long Walk to Freedom* into a three-hour film so that it captures the spirit that has amazed the world. We are willing to bet money on it that he will master this challenge in the same calm, deliberate way that he has mastered everything else in his life.

How Felicia Mabuza-Suttle's faith got South Africa talking

Faith is the essential ingredient of confidence, without which even the most talented person will disintegrate. And love her or hate her, you can't ignore Felicia Mabuza-Suttle. Mike appeared on her TV show when she addressed the subject of depression. He was stunned by the impact of her programme, especially among black women. It seemed that every black woman in South Africa with access to a TV set had watched the programme. Felicia maintains that she reaches about six million people with her show, and we can well believe it. When we interviewed black women and asked them why Felicia is so popular with them, they replied that Felicia was their role model because of her confidence, common touch and aura of caring. They also said that they love Felicia so much because she has the guts to tackle the issues that are most real to them. Most of them said that whatever they were doing or wherever they were, everything was put on hold while they watched her show. On Power Talk, Felicia shared the following insights into herself with Mike.

'I was born in Sophiatown before the government's policy of forced removals took us to Soweto. I was brought up by my grandparents. They taught me to be a proud little Shangaan girl, despite the fact that Shangaans were looked down upon at that time. I was brought up to believe I was the child of kings and queens. I think that is where my confidence comes from. I know many people call it arrogance. But it's not arrogance: it's just this little girl from the dusty, dangerous, daring streets of Soweto who really has faith in herself. Also, confidence in our African culture is sometimes seen as arrogance. But you know what, if I were a man who had a go-getter attitude, I wouldn't be described as arrogant. I would be described as normal. Part of the challenge facing South Africa as I see it, is to overcome the PHD syndrome that so many people have. PHD stands for Pull Her Down. We have to learn to celebrate other people's success. I want to be successful, I want to make money and I'm not going to apologise for that. I have learned to live with criticism. In fact, I compare myself with a tennis ball: you bounce me, I bounce back; you bounce me harder, I bounce back even higher.

'But what I really want to do is to get South Africans talking. When I first had the idea for 'Top Level', I thought South Africa was really hungry for a forum where we could all come together, black and white, young and old, and start talking to each other about real issues. But my vision was to get ordinary people on the show so they could air their views, and not the so-called experts who appear to know everything. That's why you won't see big shots on the Felicia show. You'll see everyday people talking about prostitution, gays, affirmative action, rape, domestic workers, depression, suicide, homelessness. I am trying to get people to share what is in their hearts and in their minds, so that the millions of people watching them don't feel alone in their struggle. I've had dramas on my show that make anything else on TV look tame. One of the most moving experiences for me was a young model who appeared on the show who told me how she had held back from telling her story before. But after watching me trying so hard to bring issues out into the open, she agreed to tell the nation her story. She spoke about how she had been drugged and raped repeatedly as a young model. Then she broke down. It took a lot of guts for her to do it, but it was also something she desperately needed to do. By telling her story, I think she also communicated a very valuable message to many young people.

'So yes, I want to be successful, but I also want to make a difference. I want to say to all the black women in this country, I am your sister, I am your mother, I am your friend, let's talk about it. We have the right to do that.'

How Don Ncube's faith transformed anger into energy

Don Ncube is one of South Africa's most powerful business people. As chairman of New Africa Investment Holdings, he controls a company with a market capitalisation of R6 billion. He tells his remarkable story of how he learned to transform his anger into energy.

'I was born and bred in Alexandra. At that time, the only division between Alex and Sandton was Louis Botha Avenue, which today is called Pretoria Main Road. I think what inspired my aspirations was seeing what other people had every time I looked across the road. I don't regret growing up in the environment of Alex, because in a place like that you learn very quickly to survive. You learn to live by your wits. You learn to somehow make ends meet. You also learn to do whatever it takes to make money. As kids, we used to go around picking up old tins that we sold as scrap metal; we used to caddie; we used to do any job, no matter how menial, to put money into our coffers. And all the time we were inspired by the environment across the road. Somehow, despite apartheid, I always believed it was possible to get there. It took me 38 years to cross the road and come live in Sandton and yet I was born right next to it.

'Obviously I was angry at the system. But I used the anger to do things for myself and change the circumstances that surrounded me. My anger manifested itself in energy. And I harnessed the energy to become self-reliant and shape my future, rather than to just sit and commiserate with others about the oppression designed to keep us down. I think my anger motivated me to stand up and move forward. Because if you return anger with anger, two wrongs will never make a right. I've taught myself to smile. Some would say I smile too much. But I believe that you need to have the capacity to laugh at yourself and the world around you. Only then can you prevent yourself from becoming a hopeless, helpless invalid. One of my role models was Steve Biko and somehow Steve Biko always managed to smile. Now my mission is to help other people, especially kids, to transform their anger.

'In the past, when kids saw a successful person in the townships, they associated him with either sport or entertainment or with corruption and crime.

They never associated successful black people with formal business, because we were prevented from becoming part of formal business by apartheid. Even today, when you ask kids in the townships which are the most important occupations or careers, they will say teachers, lawyers, doctors and perhaps politicians. But they will never say business. There is always the suspicion that a businessman must be doing something sinister or something bordering on the corrupt. I think it will change, but I think it will take five to ten years before there are enough successful, ethical black businesspeople to change their perceptions. So I am a champion of successful black people. And I'm proud that we have, through our shareholding, something like 1,2 million individuals of all colours participating in the wealth created by my company.' Hey, that's not bad for a kid from Alex.

How Hylton Appelbaum's commitment and faith helped to enable the disabled: The story of the wind-up radio

Hylton Appelbaum is the executive director of the Liberty Life Foundation, an organisation dedicated to the upliftment of South African society. He told us the following story that made us want to clap our hands in joy and incredulity. It is a remarkable testimony to the power of ingenuity, determination and goodwill between nations.

'The story of the wind-up radio begins with a British inventor, Trevor Baylis. Baylis had a flash of inspiration while watching a TV documentary on the Aids pandemic in Africa. The programme outlined the difficulty of communication and the consequent lack of health education in most of Africa. We came to hear of Baylis's first experiment with a wind-up radio that could work without batteries, and we were immediately fascinated by the potential of the product. Most South African homes in the rural areas are still without electricity. What's more, batteries themselves are not only very expensive but are virtually indestructible pollutants. Radio is very important for communication, education, culture and entertainment — and a key to effective development. But the largest barrier to radio's widespread use has always been the cost and availability of providing a means of power.

'I became very excited about the possibility of a radio powered by a hand-wound motor. It would eliminate the problem of access to power and give many of our poorest people access to the information they need to improve their lives and to safeguard their families. Liberty Life Foundation has long had a successful involvement in the distance education field, albeit in television, and with this project, we began to investigate further the potential of radio.

'The British government, through their Overseas Development Administration (ODA), provided a substantial grant and we decided to take a two-pronged approach. Firstly, we established a trust to help fund the development of the radio. What's more, any profits made by the trust from the sale of the wind-up radio are ploughed back into educational programmes for both radio and TV. Secondly, we established a company, Disability Employment Concerns (Pty) Ltd (DEC), which would be owned in equal shares by democratically elected bodies representing South Africa's disabled people.

'DEC's prime objectives are to create real employment for disabled people who are not satisfied with pointless labour in sheltered workshops. Why should people spend countless hours weaving baskets for which there is no market, when they could be earning real wages making hi-tech goods that are in great demand all over the world?

'Well, I am thrilled to say that the wind-up radio has become an unqualified success. DEC now has 130 employees, including the deaf, the blind, the physically and mentally disabled and fully abled people. DEC employees now feel differently about themselves. They have earned respect in the eyes of their families, their friends, and, perhaps most importantly, themselves. In fact, DEC's factory in Cape Town is currently working overtime and recruiting a larger workforce to change to a double-shift system. Not only has this enterprise a social soul and noble objectives, but it is creating millions of dollars in export earnings for South Africa. We are on track to a turnover of R40 million in our first year! What's more, the productivity of these people exceeds that of many private enterprises staffed entirely by the abled.

'DEC's chairman, Dr William Rowland, may be blind but he is a visionary. At his suggestion, a staff share trust is currently being created for DEC's employees. They will, therefore, share in some of the advantages of equity ownership. Dr Rowland's vision is one of true empowerment.

'Our initial partner was the British government, but private enterprise has also played its part. Gordon Roddick of the Body Shop plc, one of the world's leading retailers and arguably the world's most ethical and socially committed company, has invested in this project and now owns equity. British prime minister John Major said on the opening of the factory in Cape Town, "I am proud that the wind-up radio's development has been such an outstanding example of collaboration between Britain and South Africa."

'I believe that countless further jobs will be created and an increased level of profits will flow into the company and the NGOs it represents when we bring the wind-up torch and other electronic goods to market.'

All we can say, Hylton, is 'WOW!' What a paradigm shift — from handout-recipients to highly productive generators of value-added products and foreign exchange earnings. It begs the question: who is really the disabled person? We believe it is the person without the capacity for faith and wonder or the ability to follow through. What was that story about the mustard seed...?

How Stan Katz's vision and love for radio helps him beat the burnout

Stan Katz, the chairman of Primedia Broadcasting, the holding company for 702 Talk Radio, tells of his ongoing battle against burnout in his quest for success.

'I used to be invincible,' he says with characteristic disc jockey humour, 'until I discovered it was more fun breaking down. Seriously, though, I dip in and out of burnout. But what has always kept me going is this vision to pioneer the power of radio in this country. The worst period of burnout I experienced was when I was fired as the programme director of Swazi Radio. I wanted to be the general manager, but the existing general manager wasn't yet ready to relinquish his job, so I was thrown out. For a while I couldn't get a job in radio and that was the kiss of death for me. I couldn't eat lunch in this town. But I did whatever I could to stay close to radio. I went into advertising. I managed a rock band. I staged rock concerts.

'But I never lost the dream. I never lost the burning desire to crack it in radio. Now that I have cracked it, I'm terrified of losing it. I'm probably a little more cautious now, because I've seen how fast it can all disappear.

'I remember when I started off as a disc jockey. I was working 25 hours a day. I had just broken up with a girlfriend of six years' standing. I would sometimes drive to my show crying. But the moment I hit the mike switch, I became "Happy Stan, the doctor of love". For those three hours, I would put aside my misery and focus single-mindedly on what I was doing. Those three hours were my therapy. That time on air is what got me through that black period.

'The weird thing, though, is that I was afraid that my creative spark would desert me if ever I lost my misery. I thought that my misery was my edge. My misery drove me. But as I've matured, I've discovered that my productivity soars when I'm at peace, when I'm not abusing myself, when I'm exercising and meditating. My challenge now is to sustain those periods of inner calm.'

How Greg Blank's mental toughness helped him to survive prison

Mike is a friend of Greg Blank, the stockbroker who spent almost two years in prison because of fraud. During Greg's incarceration, Mike visited him frequently. Each visit was an inspirational experience for Mike, because of Greg's ability to rise above his circumstances and focus on the positive attributes of his experience.

If you've ever been inside a prison, you'll know it is a hellish place. Mike was chilled every time he entered Krugersdorp Prison where Greg served his sentence. As you are directed through the heavy metal gates guarded by wardens and their Rottweilers, you enter another world; a world without compassion or tenderness; a world populated by men who have scarred and been scarred by life. Part of Mike's core beliefs is that people are miracles; that every human being has the god within him; that people are inherently decent. So he found it especially frightening to be in a place filled with people who are paying the price for hurting, even killing, other people. The drab olive-green uniform is worn by the prisoners like a badge of shame and their eyes reflect their humiliation and anger. It was into this world that millionaire Greg Blank was thrust.

During all his conversations with Blank, however, Mike never once heard him bemoan his fate. He took total responsibility for his actions that lead him to prison. Blank was completely free of the one emotion that disempowers so many people: self-pity. 'When I got here,' Blank told Mike, 'I knew I had to do something to leverage myself into a more favourable position. As an affluent white prisoner, I was particularly vulnerable. So I raised funds from my contacts on the outside to improve the sports facilities inside the prison. But then I discovered a higher purpose: I wanted to improve the entire facility for the well-being of all its inmates.'

Blank applied his energy and ingenuity to introduce a range of initiatives that transformed the prison. These initiatives ranged from setting up a recreation committee, to commissioning prisoners with artistic ability to paint colourful murals on the drab prison walls, to establishing a prison band, to getting in guys like Mike to deliver motivational talks and donate books, to setting up a hair salon and providing television sets with M-Net.

Watching Blank at work in the prison was like watching a masterful managing director lead his company. During Mike's two-hour visits with Greg, tens of people would approach him with queries and requests for advice. Mike marvelled at the way Greg handled each one with calmness and courtesy. 'I made a decision that I was going to make the most of my experience. I was going to make a difference. I was going to get stronger, not weaker, in prison. I was going to focus on what I could achieve, not on what would depress me. I saw too many people who were broken by the prison experience.' Mike joked with Greg that he had introduced so many innovations into Krugersdorp Prison that he probably had head office worried. Even after his release, Blank is so committed to his work in the prison that he is determined to continue with his contributions. 'Too much energy and effort went into it to give up,' he says.

After his release from prison, Blank told the press that 'Jail may turn out to be the best experience of my life. You don't realise what you have until you lose it. You realise just how little you need to survive. On the outside you get involved in your own importance and you start thinking you are a god. Then you end up in jail and you realise you are no one. I was dealing with millions of rands every day, but I had to go to jail to find out what money is really worth. A rand in jail is like R100 on the outside. You have no idea what a guy will do for R1. He will sell whatever he has, including his body, if he needs something badly enough. Do you know what it is like not having to wear green clothes? I have learnt the true meaning of freedom: just being able to walk around without being confronted by a gate every ten metres. Human values of friends and family are not things one recognises when cocooned in luxury. Prison brings one face to face with a desperate reality. I'll never take anything for granted again.'

The determination and resilience of everyday South Africans

You're probably saying to yourself, 'It's all very well for Lascaris and Lipkin to quote all these extraordinary people and their extraordinary achievements, but what about me? I'm just an ordinary person trying to get through each day. Of what relevance is all of this to me?' Well, that is the magic of our rainbow nation. The rainbow nation is making progress not because of the pseudo-heavyweights at the top, but because of the determination and resilience of everyday South Africans.

Barbara and Christine just did it

The people who have inspired us the most are those individuals without power or privilege who decided to seize the day and live their dreams. One of those people is Barbara Heyburgh. Barbara was a marketing representative for a leading healthcare company. She is in her mid-thirties, divorced with two children, with no financial support from her husband. Barbara had worked for this company for over ten years. She was earning a good salary, but she wanted more: she wanted to run her own business. She had a range of marketing skills that would empower her to achieve her ambition — but she was too scared to leave the comfort zone of a large corporation. A motivational workshop we did with her company was the spark that she needed. The following week, Barbara and her cousin, Christine Searll, made the decision to go out on their own; and they started a company called Cousins Incorporated which would specialise in organising corporate events and conferences in Cape Town. It's not as though Barbara wasn't scared to do so. She told me that she was terrified. She had no safety net and very little capital. But she told me that it was a delicious feeling: it was the feeling of being alive, of being the person who Barbara Heyburgh was meant to be. A year and a half later, Barbara and Christine's business is thriving and Barbara is living her life to the max.

Go, Solly, go

Solly Krynauw was a manager of a Mitchell's Plain liquor store which belonged to a massive chain. After attending one of our sessions, he made up his mind to buy an independent bottle store that was for sale near where he lived. He had always dreamed of working for himself, of being the 'boss'. However, Solly was 52 years old and he sure as hell didn't have the cash to buy the store. He remortgaged his small house, begged and borrowed from friends and family, and made a deal with the seller to pay the seller a part of the selling price out of the store's profits over the following year. Solly now has three stores. What is more, he has built his mini-empire in just two years. Solly, if you are reading this: boykie, we are proud of you! Solly's dream just goes to show that if you can dream it, if you want it with all your heart and soul, you *can* do it.

Allison's story

Allison was an insurance representative in Port Elizabeth. She led a quiet, stable, unremarkable life. Until the night she was abducted by two men who dragged her into the bush, raped her repeatedly, stabbed her 27 times and slit her throat. Somehow she managed to drag herself to the road where a passing medical student gave what first-aid help he could and took her to the nearby hospital. Allison survived and her story has been told throughout the national media. Allison is becoming one of the country's most powerful public speakers. Her theme is that we all have a choice about how we see what happens to us. Mike met Allison and was enchanted by her calmness and serenity, but what really blew him away was when Allison said to him, 'If I could go back 18 months and could somehow have prevented what happened to me, I'm not sure I would have. Because it took that traumatic experience to make me realise my personal power and what I'm really capable of doing. Through my experience, I am now empowered to help so many people.' For us, Allison represents the ultimate expression of faith and the power of love. If you ever get the chance to listen to her, don't miss it. She is living proof that people have more strength than they know they have. That is why it often takes extreme pressure or a traumatic experience to reveal our true power. Remember: a diamond is coal made good under pressure.

How Thembi Buthelezi's faith in hard work produced miracles

Thembi Buthelezi is an unassuming, quiet 42-year-old woman who was interviewed by Mike on Power Talk. Thembi is the principal of Soweto's Reasoma Secondary School. *Reasoma* is a Northern Sotho word that means 'We work hard.' She was invited to appear on the show because of the miraculous results she achieved with her matric students in 1995: 98 per cent of her students passed, against a national average of just more than 50 per cent.

The steel in Buthelezi's character revealed its glint when Mike asked her about the secret of Reasoma's success. Reasoma does not have more resources, more teachers or better facilities than any other of the severely underfunded schools in Soweto. So how did she achieve such remarkable results — results so extraordinary that she was profiled in *Newsweek* magazine as a miracle worker? Thembi Buthelezi says with soft intensity, 'I don't want to disappoint the nation. I feel a huge commitment to each and every one of my students. I want to help them rise above their circumstances, so that they can fulfil their true potential. I want them to make their parents proud. And when they succeed, they give their parents the joy of seeing their children achieve what they couldn't. That's why I also involve the parents in setting goals for the children. Without the parents' participation, the students can't thrive.

'At Reasoma, we have also established strict rules of behaviour. Any student who breaks these rules is expelled or suspended. Without discipline, there can be no progress. We lock our gates all day to keep out drug dealers and other undesirables. But I think the biggest reason for our success is the quality of the teachers we have managed to attract. I think that I have the greatest teaching staff in South Africa. All 40 of us are totally dedicated to success. If teachers and principals work together, there is no way that pupils can be a problem. Here we work as a team, and we've been able to inculcate the discipline we dreamed of. It also helps that Reasoma is a new school. We have no baggage here, just a common goal: to achieve a 100 per cent pass rate among our matric students.' If history is anything to go by, there is a 100 per cent chance that Thembi will achieve her goal.

Thembi Buthelezi is an exhilarating example of the power of passion. When she talks, there is no ranting and raving. She is almost embarrassed by the attention her school has received. Buthelezi's passion is like a slow, relentless burn. She simply does not entertain the possibility of failure. She says that she's been through too much not to achieve her goals. All of us should be imbued with the spirit of Thembi Buthelezi.

You don't believe what you see, you see what you believe

If faith is the master conviction, what are the other contributing beliefs that fire up South Africa's champions to become great? Through our contact with hundreds of this country's most highly effective people, we have identified the ten core empowering beliefs that differentiate them from the crowd. As you read through these beliefs, ask yourself whether you share these personal truths. That is what a belief really is: your personal truth. It is your feeling of certainty about something. All truth is relative; if you believe something to be true, then it is true. That is why we eventually become our beliefs. Beliefs are the filters through which we process all our experiences. You don't believe what you see; you see what you believe. It is not the experience that determines who and what you become; it is the truth that you extract from it. Extract a bitter truth, and you become bitter; extract an encouraging truth and you become courageous. The following ten core empowering beliefs of Champion South Africans will help you achieve just that.

The ten core empowering beliefs of Champion South Africans

First core empowering belief: They have a sense of mission, a calling that draws them like the river to the sea. They are in focus and they are in flow.

Second core empowering belief: They are in charge of their own destiny. They have the power to change the world around them. They know that it is not what happens to them that is important; it is what they do about it.

Third core empowering belief: People are inherently good and worthy of their trust. Every person is unique and every person is a miracle.

Fourth core empowering belief: Even though they may not be religious, they are all spiritual. They use their higher power to guide them. They have learnt to trust themselves.

Fifth core empowering belief: They have been put here to make a difference to the people around them. They are interdependent: they take care of themselves by taking care of others.

Sixth core empowering belief: There is no failure, only feedback. Everything that happens to them serves them. There is no such thing as a good or bad experience — only the learning they take from life.

Seventh core empowering belief: The person with the most flexibility in thinking and behaviour has the most chance of succeeding. They let go of what does not serve them any more and wholeheartedly adopt what does. *They know that only the coward never backs down.*

Eighth core empowering belief: They put themselves on the line every day. They make themselves vulnerable. There is no such thing as an excuse: they take personal responsibility. They control their own emotions.

Ninth core empowering belief: Life is a neverending adventure into the future. Every day brings with it something new to get excited about.

Tenth core empowering belief: They like who they are and what they are becoming. They trust their intuition. On the surface it may sometimes appear as arrogance, but it really is a deeply ingrained confidence.

It is time to design your own personal blueprint to make you a Champion South African. But first you need an instinctive belief that you were meant to do great things

All successful companies have a business plan, a blueprint for the future. They have a vision, mission, values, measurable objectives, a strategy for achieving those objectives and tactics for achieving their strategy. Without this indispensable guide, they know they will flounder about without direction.

Yet, when we ask the vast majority of people about their personal blueprint, they look at us blankly.

'A personal blueprint?' they respond. 'We don't need that.'

'Okay,' we answer, 'then what is the most important thing that you want to achieve?'

'We want to be successful,' they say.

'What does being successful mean?' we ask.

'You know,' they reply vaguely, 'money, position, happiness and all those kinds of things.'

Well, here is what we *do* know: if you do not have a clearly defined personal vision, you have double vision. If you do not have an explicit target, you'll never hit it. And if you do not know where you're going, you'll never get there. *Clarity is power.*

You may be heading for it, or you may already be suffering from what we have branded the Victoria Falls Syndrome. It is something that both of us have been through. The Victoria Falls Syndrome is when you wake up one day and you are a few feet from the edge of the falls. As you hear the thousands of tons of water hit the rocks below, you ask yourself: 'How the hell did I get here?' If this sounds familiar, it is time to focus on your future

Wendy Luhabe, entrepreneur, wife of Sam Shilowa and managing director of the highly successful human resources consultancy Bridging The Gap, doesn't believe in forecasting. She believes in what she calls backcasting. Instead of basing your future on your past, she says, you need to project yourself into where you want to be, and then work backwards from there. Are you future-focused? Do you have a picture of your future that excites you? Is your future the kind of place that you want to live in? Or are you driving through the fog, barely able to see beyond the next few moments?

We talk to many people who are afraid to even start defining their vision. Have you ever noticed how we put off and put off those tasks that appear to be difficult, painful or awkward, often until we have no choice but to perform the task before we are hit with adverse consequences? Why do you think we are called pro-crastinators, not amateur crastinators? You see, having a personal vision never becomes urgent. Without a personal vision, we continue to exist and survive — but it's a grey version of the existence that we are capable of living.

If you have read this far, you are the kind of person who is determined to design a compelling future irrespective of what happens around you. You may not even know it yet, but you have taken a huge step forward — you have taken action, you have become aware of the need to chart your own course. The moment that you begin thinking through where you are going is when you begin to influence where you are going. Everything is created twice: events are first created in our minds and then they are created in reality. Almost every

Champion South African started out with only an instinctive belief that they were meant to do great things. From somewhere deep inside of them, they knew that they were put on this planet to make a difference. We are talking about the first, second and fifth core empowering beliefs of Champion South Africans. And it is not something that originates in the head: it is something that rises from the soul, acquires the impetus of the emotions and, finally, the clarification of the intellect.

Our purpose in including the preceding sketches of achievement was to instil in you a personal sense of greatness. No matter where you have come from, or where you are, or how long you've been here, your personal sense of greatness will empower you to take risks that you may have been afraid to take before. Time and time again, we hear people who have made it, or who have taken their first leap of faith, say: 'I don't know why I waited so long. I should have done this a long time ago. I can't believe all the obstacles I put in my own way.'

Are you burning your way through life? Or is life burning you…?

We are not talking about changing the world. We are not saying that all of us have the potential to become a Mandela or a Gandhi or a Mother Teresa. What we are saying is that all of us have the potential to become the most that we were meant to be. We are saying that all of us have a genius inside. We have the ability to do one thing incredibly well: we all have the ability to positively impact our immediate circumstances. And when we use the word 'genius', we are not using hyperbole. We are continually delighted by the phenomenal achievements of everyday people — once they have discovered their unique gift. The tragedy is that many people never discover or develop their genius. We spend our lives hiding from ourselves and disguising who we really are to other people. It is not that life is so short, it is that we wait too long to really begin living it. It is written that when we go up to meet our Creator, He asks us only one question: 'Were you you? Did you discover your purpose and live your life accordingly?' The spirit of what we are saying here was movingly expressed by the quote that concluded the film 'Schindler's List': 'He who has saved one life has, as it were, saved the world entire.'

One of the saddest stories we would like to share with you is an experience that Mike had one day, just before he was due to deliver a keynote address to celebrate the merging of three computer companies to form a R1 billion corporation. Mike was standing in the lobby of the conference centre waiting for the event to start. Being a motivational speaker, he is predisposed to talk to anybody within earshot. He noticed a woman standing by herself in the corner, looking quite melancholy. He approached her with the following opening line, 'Hi, Janet [everyone was wearing a name tag], you must be very excited about the possibilities of your company with this merger!' He was taken quite aback by her response: 'No,' she said, 'you don't know the difficulties that I've been through over the past year. I can't get excited about anything any more.'

Janet did not have a sense of future, she only had a sense of the past. She was focused on the pain or the injustices of what she had been through. The more she focused on those perceived personal injuries, the more psychologically wounded she became. We are not asking Janet to repress or forget her perceived injuries, but Janet, if you are reading this, please forgive both yourself and whoever injured you. We are asking you to squeeze the learning out of your experiences. Identify your fears and recognise the signals they are sending you. Move forward. By staying where you are, you are only hurting yourself.

We would like to help you build your personal blueprint to become a Champion South African. If you are one of the rare people who already have a blueprint, use this section to take stock, and to refine your personal blueprint so that it becomes even more powerful.

What we have discovered through our own experience is that a written personal blueprint provides a focal point for our energy. It is the difference between the energy of the sun and the energy of a laser beam. The sun's energy is broadly dissipated over everything. The laser beam's energy is a pure concentration of light on a specific element. Result? The laser beam can burn through even a diamond. Try this exercise (which is probably something that you did as a child): buy yourself a magnifying glass, and then use the magnifying glass to concentrate the energy of the sun to a pinprick of light against a piece of wood. Watch as this pinprick of light burns its way clear through the wood. Are you burning your way through life? Or is life burning you?

Think BIG

Before we discuss the Seven Questions of Faith, we ask you to think BIG. BIG is an acronym for *Bold Inspiring Goal.* Your personal blueprint is a vision of the kind of person that you aspire to become. Your personal blueprint must be bold and inspiring: it is, after all, the all-encompassing goal that you move towards every day. Even though your personal blueprint is an aspirational contract with yourself, write it in the present tense, as though you were living it now. That gives it an immediacy and urgency rather than making it something that you contemplate doing at some point in the future.

Webster's Dictionary has an exhilarating definition of 'boldness': 'not hesitating in the face of possible danger; necessitating courage and daring; challenging; imaginative; beyond the usual limits of conventional thought or action'. If there is one word that sums up the essence of Champion South Africans, it is their boldness according to this definition. Do you have boldness? Or are you tentatively tip-toeing your way through life? Make sure that your personal blueprint has boldness in it. We agree with Goethe when he said, 'Whatever you can do, or dream you can, begin it. Boldness has genius, power, and magic in it.'

Webster's Dictionary has an equally rousing definition of 'inspire': 'to guide or control by divine influence; to infuse with an animating, quickening or exalted influence'. We believe that when you are inspired, you are tapping into the energy of your higher power; you are elevating yourself to the next level, you are amplifying your personal energy to make great things happen. Neither of us is religious in the conventional sense, but we both have a powerful belief in a force that is greater than us, a force that has come to our aid time and time again. We have experienced the power of miracles, learning and good fortune too often to believe that life is a series of random occurrences. There is no such thing as coincidence. Whatever happens has to happen. But you can influence what happens by your faith, energy and goals.

Webster's Dictionary's definition of 'goal' is 'the result or achievement toward which effort is directed'. Not having Big Inspiring Goals, therefore, is like starting a hot dog in the middle: you end up in a mess.

Mike Lipkin's and John de Florio's personal blueprint

The most effective way we can guide you as you answer your own Seven Questions of Faith is to share a couple of personal blueprints with you and discuss how we learnt to think BIG. Our personal blueprints are fluid. We are constantly reshaping them as we climb to our personal peaks. In this sense, our personal blueprints are like the Japanese concept of kaizen: constant and neverending improvement. The moment we stop improving, we start dying.

Our personal blueprints are our constant compasses. They are the reference points that keep us focused and directed. They are also our daily dose of inspiration. They express the best that we are capable of being. When the helter-skelter of everyday life in South Africa threatens to engulf us, our personal blueprints give us perspective. As you read through Mike's personal blueprint, therefore, please do not regard it as arrogant or boastful. It is simply the description of who he is trying to become every single day. It is the expression of his most desired aspirations. That is why he has written it in highly inspirational language: he uses it every day to rev himself up.

To succeed in life, you have to walk your talk. The core message of Mike's talks and workshops around the world is the need to 'know thyself': if you do not know what drives you, how can you presume to know what drives anybody else? If you are operating from a base of personal uncertainty, how can you focus single-mindedly on helping others? How many times have you been in a meeting with someone where there is so much noise going on in your head that you cannot hear what the other person is saying? Have you ever noticed how, when you have uncertainty inside you, the other person can sense it immediately? Our feelings are infectious. Other people catch our emotional viruses. You cannot fake inner strength and certainty, the kind of certainty that only a personal blueprint can give you. Mike has invested much in his personal blueprint: it is his mental, emotional and spiritual software.

John de Florio is a mutual acquaintance of ours who lives in Los Angeles, California. John is one of the most effective people we know. He is a 'performance coach' to many of California's leading companies where he helps to transform managers into leaders. We have featured de Florio's personal blueprint here because it represents such a superb balance between his business and personal objectives.

So, use Mike Lipkin's and John de Florio's personal blueprints as benchmarks for your own personal blueprint. But be sure to write yours in such a way that it inspires and motivates you every time that you look at it. All that we can do here is to help you start your engine. You have to keep your motor running. You have to get out there on the highway. You have to have your own adventure. You have to turn whatever happens to you to your advantage.

Mike Lipkin's personal blueprint

Purpose
To passionately inspire, educate and empower the people around me to constantly improve the quality of their lives and the lives of all those they have the privilege to touch.

Identity
I am the most effective and passionate communicator of influence training in the nation. I am a force for personal and interpersonal good. I am an outrageous, response-able, funloving, compassionate, reassuring, coaching, exciting, pioneering, bold, proactive person.

Core beliefs

I'm here to make a difference by learning, growing and passionately sharing. Life is a gift. People are miracles. The deeper my friendships, the more joy and success I experience. If I meet people's true needs with total sincerity and commitment to serve, they will consistently do business with me. My work is pure magic. I am blessed. I am the luckiest person I know. The secret to living is giving. I am guided. Everything that happens serves me.

Values

Health, freedom, growth, contribution, love, adventure, passion, making a difference.

Behaviour

I live with passion. I seize every opportunity to learn. I spread humour and laughter. I smile often. I hug people. I seek first to understand, then to be understood. I constantly improve my relationships through continuous emotional deposits. I always go for the win-win. Every day, I cultivate my attitude of gratitude. I expand my impact through my reputation based on my actions and effective communication through the media. I touch the sky by encouraging my imagination to soar. I give people all my positive energy. I catch people doing things right.

Strategic plan

☛ Develop quality relationships with the 'Lipkin 200'.
☛ Stay top-of-mind by constantly featuring in the media.
☛ Create one major new programme or book every year that sustains my self-directioning as a pathfinder.
☛ Consistently benchmark myself against the finest communicators in the world.
☛ Expand my circle of contacts to ensure I am relevant to every South African.
☛ Surround myself with strategic partners who are the best of the best.

One-year goals

☛ Deliver 250 talks/workshops.
☛ Stage ten major public events.
☛ Achieve R5 million in turnover.
☛ Achieve spontaneous awareness among major prospects.

☞ Be acknowledged by my target customers as South Africa's Number One motivator.

John de Florio's personal blueprint

Purpose

To consistently fill people with a sense of optimism, confidence and encouragement so that they can make the impossible possible.

Identity

I am a caring and creative mentor. I am a shrewd, fun-filled person who consistently discovers unconventional ways to do what no one has ever done before. I am energised, passionate, flexible, youthful and highly intuitive.

Core beliefs

I am here to make people feel special. Leaders are dealers in hope. Life is about achieving dreams. Anything is possible. Everyone is capable of greatness. I try to be modest because life has a way of jumping up and biting you in the ass. Life is abundant with opportunities. It is a neverending adventure into the unknown. The concerns of the nation should be the concerns of the corporation. Growing old is mandatory, growing up is optional. A man's reach should exceed his grasp — otherwise, what's a heaven for? (With thanks to Oscar Wilde.)

Values

Fairness, decency, growth, family, giving, fun, flexibility.

Behaviour

I treat everyone with courtesy and respect. I challenge everything because there always is a better way. I try very hard never to lose my temper. I listen with empathy and intensity. I am always learning. I am always scheming and thinking of how to execute the next breakthrough. I develop the people around me by maximising their autonomy but I am always there to help them pre-empt crises. I ask questions no one has asked before. I act. I lead. I change what's not working. I make it easy for people to approach me.

Strategic plan

☞ I continually network with California's top movers and shakers.

☛ I build relationships with the most influential advertising and marketing people worldwide because we live in a global economy.

☛ I search for acquisitions and partnerships with exciting companies.

☛ I broaden the diversity of the people who work with me so that I am continually presented with fresh points of view.

☛ I involve myself with community projects so that I can give back.

☛ I spend as much time with my own personal board of directors — family and friends who love, support and inspire me.

One-year goals

☛ Conclude at least one major new deal that significantly expands my influence.

☛ Win at least five new clients that make my company better, not just bigger, while contributing towards making our current clients more successful than they have ever been.

☛ Become involved with a state initiative that helps me give back.

☛ Become an even better father to my children by spending more quality time with them.

☛ Get fit.

Our challenge to you

Craft your own personal blueprint by answering the Seven Questions of Faith and send it to us. We can't promise you that we shall respond to every one, but what we can promise you is this: just writing your own personal blueprint will increase your effectiveness tremendously. Make a commitment to yourself right now to write your personal blueprint and send it to us within the next 30 days. If the longest journey begins with a single step, make this the first one on your way to becoming the person you were meant to be. Start it today! If not now, when?

Okay, let's have some fun. It's time to sing. We would like you to sing a song that you probably learnt in nursery school. It's a song that sums up everything we have shared with you. (Don't be shy now. If you need help, call your nearest four-year-old to assist you.)

Row, row, row your boat,
Gently down the stream,
Merrily, merrily, merrily, merrily
Life is but a dream.

You see, you have to row your boat. Nobody else can row it for you. Go with life, go with its flow. Use its energy, don't fight it. Live merrily. It's only when we are happy that we really achieve. Dream, because ultimately our dreams make our tomorrows.

By now you have learnt to get yourself into a state of perpetual excitement; you have learnt how to let your fear energise you; you have at least started crafting your personal blueprint. You are close to achieving what Stephen Covey, author of *The Seven Habits of Highly Effective People*, calls a Private Victory. Now let's discover how you can influence other people by marketing yourself forcefully.

Four

Building your personal brand: The eight principles of personal marketing

1. What business are you really in? Think beyond your actual job.

    . . . .
    . . . .
    . . . .
    . . . .
    . . . .

2. How effective are you at influencing other people? Why?

    . . . .
    . . . .
    . . . .
    . . . .
    . . . .

3. Are you becoming more valuable over time, or are you depreciating with age? How do you know?

    . . . .
    . . . .
    . . . .
    . . . .
    . . . .

4. What do the people around you think of you? What do you want them to think of you?

    . . . .
    . . . .
    . . . .
    . . . .
    . . . .

5. Although you may be good at many things, what is the one most important benefit that you offer your customers or colleagues? What is the one benefit that you want to become famous for?

    . . . .
    . . . .
    . . . .
    . . . .
    . . . .

6. What are you doing to constantly recharge, reinvent and rejuvenate yourself?

....

....

....

....

....

7. How often do you catch other people doing things right? Do you go out of your way to compliment and praise people, or are you the kind of person who only criticises and moans?

....

....

....

....

....

....

8. Are you known as a giver or a taker? Do people come to you for solutions or advice because they know you care as much about them as you care about yourself? How can you begin giving more right now?

....

....

....

....

....

....

9. What is your level of energy? Are you a source or a subtractor of other people's energy?

....

....

....

....

....

10. How developed is your sense of humour? Does your presence evoke a grin or a grimace?

....

....

. . . .
. . . .
. . . .

Umuntu ngumuntu ngabantu: A person is a person because of other people

Umuntu ngumuntu ngabantu — a person is a person because of other people — is the golden thread running throughout this chapter. It is the code of interdependence which demands that we see ourselves in the context of our interactions with others. It means turning the concept of 'me' on its head so that we can arrive at the concept of 'we', and is the greatest challenge facing us as we move towards becoming the kind of people who have the power to influence other people.

But what is influence? A dictionary definition is 'the power of people to produce effects on others by intangible or indirect means'. If you are the kind of person who has the power to influence other people, you have the ability to impact on other people's beliefs and perceptions in such a way that they willingly change the way they look at the world and the role you play in their world. You transform the way other people think about their lives.

The first law of influence is *make it pleasurable and make it rewarding for other people to interact with you.* If you cannot persuade people to associate their most desired feelings with you, you can never reach them effectively. Who are the people who have influenced you the most? Are they not the people you really like, admire, want to be with, enjoy watching, or aspire to be? Because they make people feel good, influencers have their own brand of personal charm and charisma that draws others to them. Are you the kind of person other people like to be around? Do you leave others in a good mood? After meeting with you, do other people say, 'It's great to be with someone like that!' Or are they neutral or even relieved when they leave your presence?

Most of us are so caught up in our own problems and fears that we are deaf, dumb and blind to other people's signals. We are talking so loudly to ourselves that we cannot hear what the other person is saying. At times, we do not even want to hear what the other person is saying, because we do not believe that we can handle their message. We all know the remark, 'Don't make your problems my problems!' What are the four primary truths of influence?

If you are only concerned about yourself, the irony is that you will not be able to take care of yourself. There will come a time when you become consumed with your own anxieties and selfishness. That time may come tomorrow or it may come the next decade, but it will come. Depression is, ultimately, a form of extreme self-absorption. It attacks people who do not care for other people. Please consider this point as a *vuka*, a wake-up call. Mike learnt this lesson the hard way: he spent almost three years suffering from clinical depression.

The most valuable people and the most powerful people in South Africa today are those whom other people feel they can turn to in times of emotional need. People who have the power to reassure and motivate others have maximum influence over others. It doesn't matter what you do for a living, or where you live, or what your position is, or how educated you are: if you are the kind of person who makes others feel special by giving them affection and confidence when they need it most, you are on your way to becoming a Champion South African. In this chapter, you will discover how to apply this ability effectively. However, you have to want to do it.

You have to love yourself with a passion. If you don't love yourself, it is impossible for anybody else to love you. Have you ever noticed how uncomfortable you feel when you are with someone who is uncomfortable with themselves? Only when you love who you are can you love the people around you and genuinely communicate that love. Start practising the art of loving the person called 'you'. Focus on what makes you magic; read your personal blueprint; celebrate your imperfections. Remember: the biggest room in the world is room for improvement. We are all miracles waiting to happen; become excited about your potential.

You have to learn to use your self-love to market yourself to others. South Africans have been conditioned not to promote themselves. Somehow we believe that it is arrogant to broadcast our abilities, and therefore we undersell ourselves and suffer the consequences. We are a society that used to frown on openness and transparency. Very few South Africans have mastered the art of personal marketing. When the two of us interview people, we ask them these questions: 'What are you really good at?' 'What are your greatest strengths?' 'Why should we want to work with you?' In almost every case, the interviewee struggles to respond. By the way, what was your response to these questions?

We are not encouraging you to become boastful. We are simply asking you to identify what your real strengths are, and to learn to communicate those strengths convincingly to others.

At best, the conveyance of information is 20 per cent of the communication process; the remaining 80 per cent is the transfer of feelings and emotions

'People don't get along because they fear each other. People fear each other because they don't know each other. They don't know each other because they have not properly communicated with each other.'

— MARTIN LUTHER KING

Whatever you do for a living, you have to do it with other people. The primary skill that we all need, therefore, is the ability to communicate. However, communication skills are possibly the most underdeveloped skills of all. The old South Africa is a country that did not encourage communication; in fact, we had been dissuaded from truly expressing our points of view. As a result, we struggle to build rapport with people who come from a different segment of our diverse society. It is frightening how inadequate the communication skills of the majority of South Africans are. This holds true even for the highest corporate echelons. This section focuses on how to enhance your ability to communicate for maximum influence. However, we have expanded the concept of communication beyond one-on-one communication. We shall show you how you can build the kind of image, reputation and presence that actually draws people to you like a human magnet.

Communication is far more than just the transfer of information. At best, the conveyance of information is 20 per cent of the communication process. The remaining 80 per cent is the transfer of feelings and emotions. How you make people feel when you communicate with them will determine your ultimate success. Alfred Zeien, chairman of the Gillette Corporation, expressed this power when he said, 'We don't sell products, we capture customers.' Zeien was referring to the need not just to capture customers, but also to captivate them. That is why companies spend billions of rand every year to advertise their products and services. These products and services are promoted in such a way that people identify with them because they appeal to people's heads and their hearts. Advertising agencies invest huge amounts of time and money to understand their prospects before they create the actual advertising campaigns. Then they apply their imagination, empathy and ingenuity to create communication that captivates prospects. But even they don't always succeed. Let's consider some of the brands that have captivated South Africans. As you read through the names listed below, write down why you think they are successful:

Nando's

702 Talk Radio

M-Net

BMW

Levi's

Edgars

Woolworths

Peter Stuyvesant

Coca-Cola

Castle

These brands deliver the following benefits to their prospects:

☛ They have integrity – they are consistent over time.
☛ They are trusted to deliver quality.
☛ Their customers get a sense of pleasure from using them. They are liked.
☛ They are relevant. The brands keep pace with the times.
☛ They are perceived to be leaders in their respective markets.

Do these five points apply to you? The two of us make a living by marketing and advertising ourselves, our companies and our clients' products and services. We believe that just like Castle, Coca-Cola, BMW or Nando's, *we are all personal brands,* and that we either grow more valuable or less valuable with time.

A brand is a total value package that people want to acquire or to use because they believe that it most effectively meets their needs and desires. *Brands meet our needs through their ability to function according to our expectations. They also meet our desires through their ability to satisfy our emotional needs.* Let's look at Coca-Cola, for example. Coca-Cola meets our needs because it is a pleasant tasting, carbonated, sugared beverage that quenches our thirst. But when we buy Coke, we are really buying the millions of rand of image-building that is invested in every bottle. We are buying the promise of youth, vitality, fun, enjoyment and the lifestyle that the Coke logo has come to represent.

What about Peter Stuyvesant? Cast aside your moral considerations regarding tobacco for the moment. Look at the masterful way in which Peter Stuyvesant has marketed itself over the years. It has positioned itself as the 'international passport to smoking pleasure'. Whenever customers light up a Peter Stuyvesant, they transport themselves into the hedonistic world of the beautiful, bronzed figures that populate the Stuyvesant commercials.

Or look at Nando's. Nando's is a very young brand. It was started in 1987 with a single store in Savoy, Johannesburg. It was the brain child, and the love child, of Robert Brozin. Inspired with nothing more than a passionate love for peri-peri chicken and an evangelical zeal, Brozin took on the mighty Kentucky Fried Chicken. Today, Nando's has almost 100 outlets in South Africa and another 50 outlets around the world. It aims to have 50 outlets in the UK alone by the year 2000. When you think of Nando's, what thoughts, feelings or images do you have? How about a smile, a chuckle of appreciation, a sense that Nando's is a maverick yet lovable personality who makes a hell of a chicken?

Or consider Levi's. Have you noticed how the so-called designer label brands come and go, but Levi's just keeps getting stronger? That is because its brand values are built on the timeless principles of quality, reliability, endurance and rugged individualism. Like Castle Lager, it has stood the test of time.

What Coke, Castle, Peter Stuyvesant, Nando's and Levi's have managed to achieve is to anchor their brand image in the minds of millions of people. Every time that you see their logo, you feel a certain set of emotions. There is an instant association between the stimulus (the logo) and sensations (your emotions). We take it for granted that the product itself will perform from a functional point of view; the marketing battle is the quest for ownership of your emotions.

Now consider the following well-known South Africans and write down your immediate thoughts or feelings regarding each person:

Nelson Mandela
....
....
Winnie Mandela
....
....
FW de Klerk
....
....
Thabo Mbeki
....
....
Cyril Ramaphosa
....
....
Sam Shilowa
....
....
Dali Tambo
....
....
Francois Pienaar
....
....
Mark Fish
....
....
PJ Powers
....
....
Johnny Clegg
....
....

Felicia Mabuza-Suttle

. . . .
. . . .

Claire Johnston (of Mango Groove)

. . . .
. . . .

Just like brands, people command an emotional response from us.

☛ Nelson Mandela's profile may be that he is calm, dignified, spiritual, powerful, huggable, lovable, inspirational.
☛ FW de Klerk's profile may be that he is intense, sincere, courageous, bold, strong.
☛ Thabo Mbeki's profile may be that he is polished, urbane, charming, Mr Fix-it.
☛ Felicia Mabuza-Suttle's profile may be that she is pushy, aggressive, controversial, caring, a real character.
☛ Francois Pienaar's profile may be that he is gutsy, tough, rugged, a great sportsman.
☛ Johnny Clegg's profile may be that he is truly multicultural, exciting, talented, entertaining, energetic.
☛ Sam Shilowa's profile may be that he is stubborn, confrontational, comic.

What's your profile? What do you want people to think of you? What kind of image are you seeking to build among your clients, colleagues and friends? How are you anchoring your image in the minds of these people? This is what marketing is all about. Your profile is the way in which you package and sell yourself to the world for long-term, sustainable success — both your success and the success of the people around you.

Become a human chameleon

We are not suggesting that you try to become what you are not. In fact, if there's one primary lesson in this book, it is the necessity of being true to yourself. A person who wears more than one face eventually forgets which one is real. We are advocating that you become a human chameleon. A chameleon never forgets that it is a chameleon, but it remains focused on two primary purposes: food and self-protection. It adapts itself masterfully to its surroundings to achieve those ends. Chameleons also eat what bugs them. Decide what you need to do to adapt to the people around you: the different ways and approaches you need to maximise your influence on the people around you. Do not expect other people to adapt to you. In the eight principles of personal marketing, we'll show you how to do this.

Market yourself

We are convinced that the same principles that are applied to marketing brands can be applied to effectively market ourselves as individuals. The first step is to appreciate the need to market yourself. If you are still sceptical, we ask you to jettison your doubts until you've worked through the eight principles of personal marketing. We guarantee you that if you apply these eight principles consistently for one year, you will boost your personal success in winning friends, influencing people and making big money. If you don't, return this book to us in a year's time — and we'll refund you your money!

Are you ready to become a highly effective personal marketer? Get set, go!

The first principle of personal marketing:

The principle of perception — the thoughts and language of success

We are all bundles of flesh, blood, muscle, tissue and bone. But to other people, we are nothing but a set of thoughts and emotions. Ultimately, we are all virtual realities. We exist in the perception of other people. Our personal success, therefore, depends on how effectively we manage both our own self-perception and the perception that others have of us. Arthur Ashe, the great tennis player and human rights activist, said we are all really three people: the person we really are, the person we think we are, and the person other people think we are. However, our self-perception often becomes the perception that others have of us. Have you ever noticed that when you feel contempt for yourself, that emotion is mirrored by the people around you? When you are negative about yourself, other people become negative about you. When you are feeling good about yourself, other people begin to feel the same way.

We become what we think we are. We move in the direction of our thoughts. As Henry Ford said, 'If you believe you can do it, or you believe you can't do it, you are both right.' If there is one thing we *can* control, then, it is our thoughts. From this moment on, we encourage you to go on a permanent mental diet. Just as you should be careful about what you eat, you should be vigilant about the thoughts you allow to occupy your mind. In both of our minds, right of admission is reserved. We stand guard at the door of our minds. You cannot always control what goes on outside of you, but you can control what goes on inside your head. You can't direct the wind, but you can direct your sails: you just have to become aware of your ability to direct your sails (as well as your sales).

What are the thoughts that disempower us? We have chosen the following phrases from the thousands of conversations we have had with people over the past year. In every case, these thoughts were verbalised just before the other person made an excuse why something could not be done. As you read through these thoughts, consider whether they are part of your mental vocabulary. If they are, make a mental note never to use them again.

There's nothing I can do.
That's just the way I am.
Why does this always have to happen to me?
How come I can never get it right?
I wish this wasn't happening.
It's the way I was brought up.
I'm not creative.
I'm Italian, what do you expect?
I really tried.
They'll never accept that.
But I've always done it that way.
That's our policy.
He makes me sick.
She's driving me crazy.
It's hopeless.
What for?
It will never work.
I'll do it tomorrow.
I'm too old to change.
It's just not my day.
It's just not my decade.
It's difficult to fly like an eagle when you're working with turkeys.
It's not my fault.
I'm so worried about my future.
What's going to become of me?
I keep hitting my head against a brick wall.
It's impossible.
It's just too hard.
I can't take this any more.
He made me do it.
The devil made me do it.
I was just following orders.
I can't live without her.

> I'm at the end of my rope.
> I'll never make it.
> I'm just not smart enough.
> I'm *gatvol.*

Notice how tense these words have made you. The first person we have to learn to communicate with is ourselves. What goes on inside your head is what you eventually communicate to others through your words and gestures. If you are the kind of person who habitually uses mental phrases similar to the ones we've mentioned here, you are using words that diminish your influence over others. Prove it to yourself. Listen to the people you regard as 'losers', pessimists or negaholics (people addicted to negativity). You will hear words that drive you away from them. Companies that are struggling use a collective vocabulary of defeat; they use the language of blame and helplessness; the people there are continually searching for reasons why they are not delivering the goods. Listen to yourself. Are you using the language of the victor or of a victim? Do you excite people or do you exhaust them?

Listen to Nelson Mandela when he talks. His talk is free from the language of conflict, revenge and retribution. His spirit of humanity, hope and reconciliation is broadcast with every speech. Listen to a Hitler or a Terre'Blanche and you'll hear the language of confrontation, the language of blame, the language of hate. From this moment on, pay specific attention to the actual words that the people around you use. The most effective people, the people whom you want to follow, use words of construction and not words of destruction. Every time that you fight against something, you weaken yourself. You go against the current. Every time that you march for something great, you strengthen yourself. You go with the flow. When we hear people raging against other people, we know it's because they lack their own substance. The following anecdote about Mother Teresa illustrates our point. Mother Teresa was approached by a pacifist movement to march against war. She refused, saying the following, 'I won't march against war. But if ever you want to march *for* peace, I'll be there.'

One final tip on NegativeSpeak: there is one word that you should immediately banish from your vocabulary when you are communicating your feelings to another person: 'but'. We call it the 'eraser' word, because it erases anything else that may have preceded it. Remember the last time that you were evaluated or reviewed by your boss or a client? Remember how good you felt as they recounted your virtues or listed your personal assets? Remember what happened when they used the 'but' word to point out your shortcomings?

There is a simple solution: replace 'but' with 'and'. When you use 'and', you build on what has just been said, you don't wipe it all out.

Okay, let's get positive. Let's explore the kind of thoughts that live in the minds of people who communicate constructively with themselves and other people.

The 50 Thoughts and Phrases of Power

1. If it's to be, it's up to me.
2. I can do it.
3. I can make a difference — because I'm here to make a difference.
4. I'm a passionate, powerful person.
5. I'm gifted.
6. I'm a walking miracle.
7. I will always protect my sense of wonder.
8. I use whatever happens to me to grow stronger.
9. I'm at my best when things are at their worst.
10. Every day, in every way, I'm getting better and better.
11. What if? Why not?
12. There is always a way.
13. How come I got to be so lucky?
14. I've got no time to waste time.
15. I love this life.
16. I love this country.
17. I love the people around me.
18. I treat others with ultimate respect.
19. I love me, I am proud of me, and I like who I am becoming.
20. I'm everybody's favourite child, kind of cute and just a little bit wild.
21. I feel good.
22. I'm vertical, I'm above ground, it's going to be a great day.
23. I'll do whatever it takes.
24. I'm totally committed to making this happen.
25. I take total responsibility.
26. I never take anything for granted.
27. I'm pumped, I'm juiced, I'm jazzed, I'm magical.
28. There is no limit to what I can achieve.
29. I'm glad I'm a South African.
30. If I were any better it would be a sin.
31. What have I got to be excited about today?
32. Why should I be grateful today?

33. I find great joy in the little things.
34. What have I got to look forward to?
35. There's got to be a better way and I'm going to find it.
36. I forgive myself and I forgive you.
37. It's okay to make mistakes as long as I learn from them.
38. No one can get me down because I control my own emotions.
39. I believe in me, I believe in what I'm doing, I believe in my higher power.
40. It doesn't matter how many times I fall off, it's how many times I get back on.
41. No problem is permanent. This too shall pass.
42. Every problem is given to me to help me grow. A crisis is a gift.
43. I'm about to have a breakthrough.
44. For every boy there's a girl, for every exit there's an entrance, for every death there's a life, for every debit there's a credit, for every problem there's a solution.
45. I am not designed to be defeated.
46. I am meant to do great things.
47. The journey is the reward. There are no answers, only questions. I choose to live the question.
48. Masterpieces take time.
49. 'No' is just foreplay to 'yes'.
50. It's okay to be afraid. It's not what I feel, it's what I do that counts.

Notice how motivated these words make you feel? That is the power of the thoughts of success. Your words become the labels that you apply to your thoughts. Concentrate on turning up the volume and frequency of your positive thoughts and words while turning down the dial on your negative words and thoughts. We know that we have convinced you, so start practising the thoughts and language of success today! In fact, transfer the 50 thoughts and phrases of power featured here to a piece of paper, add your own, and constantly refer to them until they become integrated into your mental programme. You will soon find yourself breaking through those obstacles that previously would have seemed impenetrable.

If you were a product inside a package, how would you now describe yourself on the package to enhance the perception that your customers have of you? Now that you are empowered with the language of success, you may wish to revisit your personal blueprint at this stage. Try this exercise: go into your nearest liquor or cosmetics store and study the words on the packages or labels, then write your own personal sales pitch. One pitch that particularly inspired us were the words on the box containing Dimple 15-year-old Scotch whisky:

'Few whiskies attain the rare distinction of the Dimple. Over 300 years of distilling and blending experience have ensured the perfection of this most distinguished deluxe Scotch whisky. Savour the elegant taste of a subtle blend of 15-year-old whiskies that is as special as the unique dimpled bottle that holds it.' Makes you want to take a sip, doesn't it?

How to use the language of success to build great teams: The culture of achievement

'**culture:** the customs of a particular people or group'
— Oxford Dictionary

If you are the kind of person who is responsible for the well-being and performance of others, or if you aspire to this role, this is potentially the most critical section of the entire book.

Earlier on, we spoke about the language one hears in losing companies, communities or teams. Now let's look at the kind of language that permeates winning companies or teams. Language and thoughts determine the culture of a group of people. Language expresses and communicates the customs of the group throughout the organisation, team or community. However, most companies and teams stumble badly when it comes to language. The two of us see this phenomenon every day in the corporate environment. Companies are so busy trying to market themselves to their customers that they are negligent in managing the perceptions of their own people towards their company. Most of the employees do not have a clear sense of what their corporate culture is; they have even less of an idea of what their company's vision and mission is. Because of this ignorance and oversight on the part of their corporate leaders, they hire out their heads and hands — but not their hearts. It's 'just a job', a means of earning a livelihood.

A few rare corporate champions, however, understand that the customer always comes second: they understand that employees will only be motivated to serve the customer if they are being motivated by the company. Let's look at some of these corporate diamonds and how they add sparkle to employee performance. Even if you are not in a position to influence the entire culture of your corporation, you are still in a position to influence the culture of the immediate group of people you work with. Write your own culture for your business unit and use the following examples to inspire you.

One small *caveat*, though: it's not enough to have great talk, you also have to walk the talk. In all the examples that follow, management — at all levels — translates great thoughts into action. We know this because we work with all of them. Some of them are established champions, some are newcomers, some are in the process of turning themselves around. But they have all harnessed the power of passion. And, we are proud to say, they are all South African.

Nando's

We both work with Nando's. More than the actual product they sell, we believe it is their culture that has contributed most to their success. Nando's is not so much a company as a clan, with deeply ingrained myths and rituals. Mike was involved with crafting a lot of the words that follow. Read, enjoy, think, and compare the Nando's way to the way of your enterprise.

The heart of Nando's: The legend of the Barcelos cockerel

At Nando's, we believe in myth and legend. Beliefs that have stood the test of many centuries are sustained by ageless truths. Such a myth is the legend of the Barcelos cockerel. Dating back to the fourteenth century, the legend is as follows:

In Barcelos, a small town in Portugal, a passing pilgrim was wrongly accused of theft, for which the penalty was death. Feeling threatened in a foreign village, he only had his faith to call upon. He appealed to 'Our Lady' and St James (the patron saint of protection) that justice be done. The pilgrim found his way to the Judge who was to decide his fate. The Judge was about to commence eating a roast cockerel for his dinner. The pilgrim pleaded, 'If I am innocent, may that cockerel get up and crow!' The cockerel at once got up and crowed heartily. The cockerel has, to this day, been the symbol of *faith, justice* and *good luck*.

The Barcelos Cockerel has become the most visible expression of the Nando's spirit. And the heart beating in its breast is the heart of all Nandocas, the name given to members of the Nando's tribe.

The pursuit of Faith, Justice and Good Luck are the cornerstones of the Nando's constitution. At Nando's, however, we know we create our own good luck by steadfastly remaining faithful to our beliefs.

The Nando's creed

'Nando's is not about chicken. It's never been just about chicken.

It's about pride, passion, courage, integrity, and most of all, family.'

At Nando's, we know our chicken is the culmination of the process of pleasing the customer, not the beginning. Without our pride, without the passion for our calling, without the courage to blaze our own trail, without the integrity to stay true to our destiny and, most importantly, without our sense of family, we would be like any other fast food chain seeking to fill customers' stomachs.

Nando's isn't just a restaurant, it's a tradition, a culture and a way of life.

The ten basic Nando's beliefs

Since the inception of Nando's in 1987, ten basic beliefs have become ingrained in our business philosophy. We have discovered over time that if we remain faithful to these beliefs, Justice collaborates with us to achieve our objectives. These beliefs are as follows:

1. The greater the odds against us, the more determined we become to succeed. When other people say we can't, we say we can. Only by stretching can we become the best we can be.
2. There is no limit to what ordinary people can achieve if they are fired up by extraordinary aspirations.
3. Our frontline people are the real heroes of Nando's. They are Nando's to our customers.
4. At Nando's quality is not a noun, it's a way of life. We set the industry standards and then we continuously raise them.
5. There are no shortcuts. We build a solid foundation ahead of growth.
6. Nando's is all about sharing, ownership, involvement. Nandocas must hire out their hearts as well as their hands and heads.
7. We belong out in front in that place where our competition cannot follow. Our pioneering spirit is what has fuelled our success. If we lose that, we lose everything.
8. We will never compete on price. We will always compete on value. Our kind of customer will pay a slight premium for Nando's magic.
9. However big we become, we will never become a chain of clones. Each restaurant will have its own unique flavour. You have to be a true individual to be on our team.
10. Justice and Good Luck will only come to our aid if we always try and do the right thing, even when it's the hardest thing.

The Nando's way: Our people

Our people are what sets us apart from all other fast food operations. They are Nando's to our customers. They are the ones who make Nando's customers their friends. They are the basic building block for our success. That's why we need to select Nandocas so carefully.

A Nandocas is the name given to members of the Nando's family, the most special breed of people on the planet. These are the qualities that make Nandocas what they are and what they can become:

A true Nandocas has heart. It's his belief in the principles of Faith, Justice and Good Luck that makes him a champion.

A true Nandocas understands the power within himself. He doesn't follow rules, he makes his own. He knows that if he can dream it, he can do it.

A true Nandocas has a sense of pride in what he has achieved and his pride lights the way for others.

In taking care of others, a true Nandocas takes care of himself. He knows he is only as good as the people around him. He's a team player on the dream team.

A true Nandocas is an enthusiastic optimist. He is in control of his own destiny and he knows that in any problem lies a solution, which he turns into an opportunity.

A true Nandocas is true to himself because then he is true to everybody. His integrity is the source of his energy and courage.

A true Nandocas is blessed with a great sense of fun. He plays as hard as he works and he knows that laughter is the sweetest sound of all.

A true Nandocas works with the community to make a difference. He knows he must give something back to the people who consistently vote for Nando's.

A true Nandocas is a magician. He makes every customer's experience with Nando's a magical one. Because at the end of the day, he knows that's the Nando's mission.

A true Nandocas never stands still. He knows that life is a neverending adventure into the future. He remains forever young.

Kagiso Khulani Supervision Food Services (KKSFS)

Great companies are built on great ideas. KKSFS is a contract catering company that serves more than 800 000 meals every day. It is built on the idea of embodying the spirit of the new South Africa. It is a black-owned enterprise that is the result of joining together Kagiso Trust, Khulani Holdings, FirstCorp, Capital Investors, Supervision Food Services Management and the original owners, the Tongaat Hulett Group.

The chairman of the group is the remarkable Eric Molobi. Molobi states, 'Our mission, to feed the people, is both a practical response to the needs of our customers and a symbol of our commitment to develop the wider community through opportunity and empowerment. This unique venture demonstrates that black partners add value and transparency to solid businesses. It also shows that where enlightened management recognises change as a necessary element of business, a professional approach to the management of change satisfies all stakeholders.'

Molobi's vision permeates the entire company, right down to the frontline people. Mike should know: he has done extensive motivational and cultural work with the company, including assisting with the writing of the 'KKSFS North Star'.

The KKSFS North Star

We are not a company, we're a community.
We build our community by building relationships.
We feed the aspirations of our own people and the morale of our clients' people.
We serve quality that meets our clients' expectations at a price that delights them.
We are only as good as the last meal we prepare.
That's why the heroes of our community are the frontline people who make our business happen every day.

M-NET

Mike has done a lot of motivational work for M-Net. M-Net is all about bringing people the magic of entertainment. But in order to do this, they have to constantly keep the magic alive within M-Net itself. M-Net's definition of its magic is perhaps the finest definition of brand and corporate values that we have ever seen:

The M-Net Magic

Magic is a measure of the entertainment value of the M-Net offering. Our magic is constant proof that M-Net does more than just give you something to watch; it transports you somewhere you would never otherwise have visited, moving you to emotions you would never otherwise have felt. M-Net Magic turns TV watching from observation into participation.

Core brand values

Friend M-Net builds relationships with its viewers. It is never satisfied with just being a supplier of television programming. M-Net is welcome in every

home, and is the kind of friend you would unhesitatingly introduce to anyone else in your social circle. And, like all good friends, M-Net adds something
to your life — you do more, try more, experience more when you're with a
friend like M-Net, a friend who's always there for you.

Colourful Nothing is grey at M-Net. Colour is evident everywhere, even
behind the scenes. M-Net colour is more than literal, more than the opposite
of black and white. It extends to attitude, to dress, to a rainbow of programming variety. M-Net seems to devise new colours, brighter colours, primary
colours that reflect our youthful style. M-Net is incandescent. This is a
colourful country, and M-Net is brightening up the continent — and beyond.

Surprising Surprises are common experiences for M-Net subscribers, and
they're always refreshing. M-Net never drifts into rigid and formulaic conformity. Its surprises are continual: it's surprising how much there is to see on
M-Net; it's surprising how M-Net takes you beyond your normal confining
world. It is only guilty of predictability where it is necessary to enhance view-
ing ease or pleasure (eg standard programming formats). M-Net is consistent
only in the sense that you should always expect the unexpected.

Brave At M-Net, we express opinions, we take decisions, we accept responsibility. You know where you are at M-Net, and that's usually up front, at the
leading edge. Brave means adventurous, it means innovative, it means leadership, it means provocative. But it never means bland, and you know you're
never being short-changed. M-Net's passion and energy rub off on you –
making you feel braver for having experienced M-Net.

Entertaining At M-Net, we never lose sight of the fact that people watch television, above all else, to be entertained. We seek out entertainment — as
much as is humanly possible — from all corners of the world, pursuing it with
dogged determination. M-Net entertainment always touches and involves
you; always evokes a response — from laughter, joy and delight to wonder, awe
and amazement.

M-Net Magic Takes You To Another World

702 Talk Radio

As a talk show host on 702 Talk Radio, Mike feels the impact of 702's mission and value statement. It is short and muscular. And it is the spirit of 702. The station lives the mission and values outlined below.

702 Talk Radio's mission

To be a vital and necessary part of life in 702land, identifying and servicing the needs of our listeners and advertisers profitably, by providing independent, innovative entertainment, which offers a 24-hour reflection and appraisal of our changing world.

702's values

☞ Passion for who we are and what we do.
☞ Talent that delivers.
☞ Freedom of thought and expression.
☞ Re-invention and change.
☞ Honesty, integrity and credibility.
☞ Serving our community.
☞ Creativity, boldness and innovation.

Mike's Kitchen

Mike's Kitchen is in turnaround mode. After a few years of slippage, a rough dynamo named Dennis Finch has taken the helm. Dennis is one of the most passionate guys Mike knows. The following is the rallying cry that Dennis and Mike authored to restore Mike's Kitchen to its rightful place in the minds and hearts of South Africans.

Come experience the pride of the nation

You'll always get more than you expect at Mike's Kitchen. No one knows steak like Mike's. And no one serves you with more warmth and passion. We'll give you a meat-eating experience that will amaze and delight you, just like every-thing else at Mike's — the only truly South African Grillhouse.

The way of the pride

1. We always give our guests more than they expect. We make them purr with pleasure. We welcome them into our den and we bring them back again and again.

2. We demonstrate our pride in our smiles and our energy. The proof of our pride is in the highest standards of cleanliness, service, efficiency and friendliness.
3. We act with total commitment. A member of the pride does whatever it takes to make a feast at Mike's the ultimate South African Eating Experience.
4. We treat each other with courtesy and respect. When the restaurant starts pumping, we get pumped. When the heat's on, we stay in Mike's Kitchen. The greater the pressure, the better we perform. And we are only as good as each member of the pride.
5. Being a pride member is a passion, not just a job. The guest's experience is in our hands. We are all showmen and showgirls. We charm our guests through our sense of humour and personal touch.

ABSA

Mike has done extensive work with ABSA. He was delighted to discover the following 'Growth Charter' at the bank encouraging people to be proactive and develop themselves. What's more, ABSA really walks its talk. Stander Jordaan, the senior general manager charged with developing the bank's culture, frequently goes out on the in-house TV system to promote this message. It seems as though it's working.

The ABSA Growth Charter

You have the right
1. To question the way we do things and propose changes that will ensure continuous improvement in your team.
2. To voice your opinion and differ from others without being penalised in order to contribute to your team.
3. To give, ask for, receive and share information, feedback and help from anyone in ABSA in order to achieve your and your team's goals.
4. To explore and choose the best avenue of service in order to satisfy your clients' needs.
5. To experiment with new ways of doing things and to learn from your own and others' mistakes as you seek to improve your and your team's performance.
6. To seek and participate in learning opportunities (at least one hour per week) thus taking responsibility for your own growth.

These are your rights. Take the challenge and ensure your own, your team's and ABSA's growth.

Hunt Lascaris TBWA

Our vision
To be the first world-class communication group out of Africa.

Our mission
To be independent.
To create a happy and successful agency environment that attracts people who appreciate that life is too short to be mediocre.

Our values

Creativity: It's our cutting edge, our measurable point of difference.

Honesty: If we don't have honesty, we have nothing.

Urgency: Indecision and procrastination don't belong here.

Profitability: Money is not an end in itself, yet a fair profit helps us stay competitive.

Happiness: Learn to laugh (especially at yourself). Don't underestimate the power of a sincere smile.

Let us march

There is the ancient Greek myth of the two generals who sought to rally their troops for war. After the first general spoke, the troops murmured among each other, 'How well he speaks', but no one moved. After the second general spoke, the troops cried in unison, 'Let us march!'

Are you communicating with your stakeholders in such a way that they are motivated to march, or are your words gathering nothing but dust around them?

The second principle of personal marketing:
The principle of primary benefit — the world of difference is in the micro-difference

Michael Johnson won the men's 200- and 400-metre finals at the 1996 Atlanta Olympics. He became an instant legend. He won millions of dollars of endorsement contracts. He was showered with glory. The men who came fourth were just a fraction of a second slower. We don't even know their names. They won nothing but the memory of having been there.

Why do we tell you this story? We tell it to demonstrate the disproportionate reward that goes to the individual who transcends excellence to become truly outstanding. Although the difference between excellence and being truly outstanding may only be a razor thin margin, it is in this margin that true mastery is achieved.

Although we all have to be good, or even excellent, at a range of activities or skills, we have to be truly outstanding at just one of them. We all embody one primary benefit in the minds of our customers or prospects. We have to strive to be world class in this one endeavour. So many people hit their own glass ceiling and fail to fulfil their potential because they have not identified and expressed their primary benefit to the people around them: they do not differentiate themselves effectively from the hundreds of good to excellent professionals in their field of activity. They do not differentiate themselves not because they cannot do it, but because they haven't even thought about it. If this point strikes a chord with you, you need to do three things right now:

Identify your primary benefit. What are you or what can you be amazingly good at? What range of skills do you have that can be sharpened into a cutting edge? What do you absolutely love doing? Because if you don't love what you do, you'll never become a true master at it.

Develop your primary benefit to a Michael Johnson performance level. Find role models who can act as your benchmarks of brilliance and maybe even your mentors. Read, practise, learn. Become obsessed with becoming the acknowledged champion in your field. This does not require a staggering financial investment. The majority of new movers and shakers interviewed by Mike on Power Talk have zero formal education, but they seized every opportunity to learn by applying their ingenuity, imagination and determination. You have to passionately want to become a champion.

Communicate your primary benefit to the people around you. Write your own ad or produce your own brochure — even if it is just to clarify what your primary benefit is in your own mind — in compelling, motivational words. Develop your own sales pitch. If you cannot communicate your primary benefit in such a way that it makes people want to do business with you, who will ever know what you can really do? Don't sell yourself short. There are so few people who have done this very simple act that you will immediately set yourself apart from your competitors. You don't have to do this alone. If you need help, ask a friend or acquaintance who is good with words to help you. Whatever it takes, get it done. Don't procrastinate. Every moment you delay this vital task may be a lost sale, or an opportunity missed to influence someone important for future business. Remember: he who hesitates is not only lost, he is miles from the next turnoff.

Let's share with you how the two of us address the challenge of expressing the primary benefit:

Reg: 'The primary benefit of Hunt Lascaris TBWA is simple and single-minded: our creativity. Our vision statement, which we show to all our clients and prospects, states that our creativity is our cutting edge. It is our measurable point of difference. I am particularly proud, however, of one ad run by Hunt Lascaris TBWA to promote our involvement in the Peace Accord. It communicated our commitment to this country and it also communicated the true spirit of our agency.'

We've never wanted to sell anything so badly before

This ad is not about a leading brand of soup. A new, improved washing powder or the latest tennis shoes. It is about something more important. About hope. A sense of optimism.

Through our involvement with the Peace Accord, we have come to understand that at this time, more than any other, we all have to stand up and be counted. Because the more complicated things become, the more a simple solution manifests itself; it is only the individual who can bring peace.

We also understand that patiently sowing the seeds of hope takes more courage than choosing war or running away. Yet, we have to look with our hearts. And believe. For our children. For our land.

Because without optimism, we have no hope. Without hope, we have no future.

And without a future, we have nothing.

Mike: 'I know I am a very good marketer, but I am a world class motivator. I believe my primary benefit to other people, the one thing I want to stand for in the minds of my customers is my ability to excite people into action.

'I develop my skill every moment of every day by observing human interaction; by listening to people's stories; by reading almost 200 books on motivation and the human psyche over the past four and a half years — that's approximately one book a week; by attending two seminars a year in America, the home of motivational speakers, where I measure my progress against the world's best; by hosting the Power Talk show every Sunday night on 702, where I discuss the formulae for success pursued by South Africa's most powerful people; by constantly stretching myself to try new techniques and programmes; by writing one new book a year; by asking for feedback after every talk or workshop.

'I communicate my primary benefit through letters that I send to prospects and brochures that I distribute through the media promoting my public sessions. The following letter as well as my mission, my level of skill and my commitment to my clients' success appears in my brochure that advertises my Maximum Influence seminar:

From the desk of Mike Lipkin

Dear Achiever

I believe that Maximum Influence — the capacity to control our own destiny and lead others — is the single most important skill we can master to increase the quality of our lives as well as the lives of all those we have the privilege to touch.

For the past five years, I have passionately pursued the answer to what shapes human attitudes, actions and achievement. How can we create lasting change within ourselves and others? Specifically, I've focused on researching the mindsets and strategies of the most effective people in South Africa and the world. I have now formulated this learning into a set of cutting-edge personal effectiveness and marketing strategies that consistently produce extraordinary results.

I am extremely excited to have this opportunity to share with you the best of what I've learned. This programme is unlike any other seminar I have delivered. It is designed to provide you with easy-to-implement, practical self-management, leadership and selling skills to achieve your personal goals.

I commit to you that the day we spend together exploring Maximum Influence, The Power of Personal Marketing will introduce you to new levels of effectiveness, learning, passion and sheer fun.

I invite you to join me as we climb to our personal peak.

Warmly

Mike Lipkin
Your Personal Effectiveness Coach

Mike Lipkin's mission

Firstly, Mike has been to hell and back. Four years ago, Mike recovered from an almost fatal episode of clinical depression. From the heights of success, he plunged to the depths of despair. However, he believes that this experience and the subsequent recovery gave him a unique insight into the human psyche and motivation.

Secondly, he is passionately committed to being the finest communicator in the world. He travels the world to discover new, breakthough mental technologies for personal effectiveness. And he has made it his life's mission to share these technologies with the rest of South Africa.

Thirdly, he loves South Africa and all her people. He wants to empower each and every South African with the magic of Life Mastery.

Who should attend Maximum Influence?
Anyone who manages, sells to, interacts with or needs to influence others. In fact, anyone who wants to be the best they can be.

'In case you're wondering, this brochure generated a response that vastly exceeded expectations, which just goes to prove that if your primary benefit is a relevant one, and if you communicate it with passion and flair, people will respond with gusto. In fact, I hope that this book turns you on so much that you would want to listen to me deliver a live presentation on the material featured in these pages.

'You see, once you have identified your primary benefit, everything you do should contribute towards building your primary benefit in the minds of your prospects. Because of the relatively small market in South Africa, no matter how successful a book is, it can never be a real money spinner. My reason for writing this book, therefore, is not financial gain. I'm writing this book to extend my influence. I'm writing this book because of all the other opportunities that I know this book will generate. I'm being honest with you here. And honesty is the subject of the next principle of personal marketing.

'At the end of the day, the primary benefit of this book can be articulated in three words: uniquely powerful motivation. We want this book to be the most motivating book you've ever read. We hope that after reading this book, you empower yourself to do all those things you've always wanted to do but didn't.'

Get your own personal board of directors

Are you convinced about the power of the principle of primary benefit? You should be. It is your key to the magic kingdom of success. It has worked for us and it will work for you. You may wish to start the process of pinpointing your primary benefit by asking the people around you what they believe your most powerful selling points are. Treat your friends and colleagues as your personal board of directors. Use them to help you to fine-tune your primary benefit and how you communicate it. And make sure you return the favour.

The concept of a personal board of directors is not ours. It is a central feature of the Young President's Organisation (YPO) — an association of men and women who are younger than 50 and who head companies with an annual turnover of R50 million or more. Each member has a forum, a group of five to seven other members who act as their personal consultants in time of need. The value of this concept was made clear to Mike shortly after he addressed the Cape Town chapter of the YPO towards the end of 1994. One of its members is Gareth Ackerman who, at the time, was joint managing director of Pick 'n Pay. Pick 'n Pay was in the middle of a particularly combative strike action by its workers and Gareth was one of the key management decisionmakers on how to deal with the strike. He told Mike that his forum played an extremely valuable role in helping him devise the right negotiation strategy to resolve the dispute. So find the right people and use their energy and ingenuity to help you become the best you can be.

Remember, *umuntu ngumuntu ngabantu* — a person is a person because of other people.

The third principle of personal marketing:

The principle of personal honesty — people believe people who are real

Have you noticed how difficult it is to trust someone who tries to appear perfect? Have you ever felt the discomfort that comes from being with someone who can't accept and acknowledge their flaws? Have you ever felt the frustration of working with or being served by someone who refuses to admit that they are wrong?

In *Revelling in the Wild*, we said that the six most powerful words in the English language are: 'I admit I made a mistake.' We encourage people to challenge their own assumptions and beliefs because, if it's rooted in the mistakes of the past, experience can be the ultimate liability in this country.

It takes guts to confront your own imperfections and acknowledge them publicly: you have to be almost invulnerable to be vulnerable. However, the most effective people we know are people who are the first to admit their shortcomings and their screw-ups. They have come to terms with their strengths and weaknesses, and because of their self-knowledge and transparency, they are relaxed about themselves. They have also surrounded themselves with people who complement — not mirror — them. To quote the age old maxim: Honesty really is the best policy.

If you keep on trying to camouflage your weaknesses, you'll always be on edge and you'll always be afraid of someone finding out that you are not bulletproof. What's more, you'll always be on the defensive. You'll be operating out of fear, not confidence. We see this phenomenon all the time in our meetings with others. People who crave being seen as flawless have a stiffness to them; every word and gesture is affected. Their ability to engage in meaningful dialogue is restricted because they are more worried about their own image than they are about serving the needs of other people. They are terminally vain.

There are also those people who would rather say nothing than risk exhibiting their mental blemishes. Oscar Wilde put it best when he said, 'Most men lead lives of quiet desperation.' We incarcerate ourselves in our own mental prisons because of our fear of rejection. We often do not ask the kind of questions we need to ask because of the falsely perceived risk of being labelled stupid or ignorant.

The reality is exactly the opposite. Whenever you admit a negative, your client or colleague will give you a positive, especially because it is so rare. Put this theory to the test. The next time that you are with someone whom you are reasonably familiar with, admit your mistake or deficiency, instead of trying to cover it up. But don't do this in a grudging or guarded manner: admit it in a constructive spirit of goodwill. We guarantee you that the other person will respond favourably. (Obviously we are not saying that you can repeatedly screw up, admit it cheerfully and succeed.)

One of the most talked-about TV commercials in South Africa was the 'Makes you think, doesn't it?' commercial from Nedbank. It featured a serious, unglamorous banker, in his shirtsleeves in the bank's vaults. The banker turns directly toward the camera and says, 'At Nedbank, we don't offer you higher interest rates, we don't offer you better facilities, and we don't offer you bigger smiles. But a lot of people with a lot of money bank at Nedbank, a lot of top people in top positions bank at Nedbank. Makes you think, doesn't it?' This commercial was successful because it was real, it was refreshingly honest, and because it was delivered with confidence and a wry glint of humour.

One of the most touching demonstrations of honest emotion we have ever witnessed came from one of South Africa's most charismatic, popular, powerful politicians. Do you remember when Tokyo Sexwale put his head on Gill Marcus's shoulder and wept openly at Chris Hani's funeral? Did the rest of South Africa condemn him for that act? No, they took him to their heart because he revealed just how human he really is. So take off that mask right now. Flaunt your flaws. Wear your weaknesses. Direct your energy towards where it is going to have the biggest impact, not where it will simply confound and confuse you.

When was the last time you went to the circus? (If you haven't been there since forever, take someone under the age of ten the next time Boswell Wilkie comes to town.) Do you remember watching the acrobats as they performed their aerial ballet? Do you remember the heartstopping moments when an acrobat seemed to almost lose her grasp? Those acrobats could have performed their routine blindfolded. However, the director of the show knew that the true drama was in those brief moments of feigned uncertainty. Those moments made the show real.

Think about your own experience. How do you feel about people who are transparently honest, who are the first to admit their shortcomings or mistakes, who accept responsibility for their actions and immediately suggest remedial action? Here are some 'phrases of honesty' to help you on your way:

☛ You're absolutely right, I overlooked that point.

☛ You're absolutely right, my mistake.

☛ What can I say? I screwed up. But this is how I'll put it right.

☛ I apologise. It's my error/omission. I'll correct it right away.

☛ We should have checked that point. I don't know how we overlooked it, but we did. I'll make sure we address it immediately.

☛ I am not sure what you mean. Could you please repeat that?

☛ I don't know, but I'll find out.

☛ I don't often make mistakes, but when I do, it's a beaut!

☛ I understand how you must feel. I feel terrible for putting you in this situation. If we did the following, would it help?

If there is one principle that Mike has applied more than any other in his attempts to build himself as a personal brand, it's this principle of personal honesty. He claims that he is the only man in South Africa who has turned a pathology into an industry. His detractors say that he makes money out of his former misery and other people's current misery. But Mike's response is, 'All I have done is leverage my experience to illustrate the lessons I give to others. If there is one thing I've learnt about life, it's that you cannot sustain a situation that is inherently unethical or immoral. Life's great wheel of fortune soon goes round. By sharing my struggle against depression with thousands of South Africans, I know that I have made a difference in their lives. The fact that I am earning my livelihood through this is irrelevant. In any event, I don't focus on the pain — I focus on the pleasure to be derived from squeezing the juice out of every day. Literally hundreds of people have seen me sharing my experiences, and they too come out the closet and stop wasting their energy keeping their pain hidden. They see that they are not alone in the emotional challenges they face.

'But you know what I find amazing? As a child I used to stutter badly. Even now I sometimes experience a mild speech impediment, especially when I'm tired. Yet, when I do stutter in a talk, far from being critical, I feel the audience warming to me. I've reached the conclusion that being too slick can be a disadvantage, because slickness isn't real. Slickness is rehearsed, it's superficial, it's from the head, not the heart. I think that is one of the reasons why Reg has done as well as he has. He never comes across as being too smooth or glossy. He has an innate humility and almost tangible nervousness that instantly put people at ease.'

The essential ingredient of any relationship: honest confrontation

How many relationships are destroyed by the reluctance of people to bring things out into the open? How many times have you hesitated to confront someone about something they've done that has disturbed you deeply, only to look back in anger? Most people lack either the courage or the conviction to engage in what Reg calls honest confrontation.

'One of our most valued clients did something that we believed was wrong. They assigned part of their business to another advertising agency without telling us. What's more, the other ad agency used our work to promote the products they had been assigned. The first time we became aware of it was when we saw the ads in the newspaper. It surprised us because this action was so out of character with this specific client.

'However, when we first won this client a few years ago, we agreed that if ever one of us were unhappy, we would immediately discuss our concerns openly. So I called the client and we did exactly that. We talked in a spirit of honest confrontation. And we reached consensus on the issue. That meeting strengthened the relationship immeasurably because we both bared our true feelings and went to the heart of the real issues. We didn't play "spot the hidden agenda" with each other.'

Be human

To which mistakes should you admit? How can you liberate yourself by being honest about your flaws and imperfections? Be human. Other people will respond warmly to your mortality.

The fourth principle of personal marketing:

The principle of self-visualisation — dreams design our reality

'We are such stuff as dreams are made on,' said Prospero in Shakespeare's *The Tempest*. It is our dreams that inspire us to triumph over our present. Every Champion South African whom we had the privilege of speaking to has a great dream. Before you can make a great dream come true, you need to have a great dream that motivates and stimulates you, and you must genuinely believe that your dream is achievable.

Your personal blueprint is your great dream in terms of the kind of person you aspire to become, but we also need an Achievable Big Hairy Audacious Goal (ABHAG) that we want to achieve in the short term. We don't believe in five-to-ten-year goals in this country. If, in South Africa, you don't win in the short term, there is no long term. As John Maynard Keynes said, 'In the long run, we are all dead.' Your ABHAG is the tangible result of living your personal blueprint; it is the material expression of your success; it is the equivalent of hitting the bull's-eye of your most desired target.

Your personal blueprint and your ABHAG become your self-visualisation. Your self-visualisation is your compass when you venture into the unknown. We talk to so many people who are afraid of the future. They are confused, they feel like they're adrift, they have no momentum, they're just treading water. In most cases, they feel disempowered because they haven't crafted their personal blueprint or consciously focused their psychological and mental energy on their ABHAG. Because they don't know the end of their personal movie, they are living their lives in uncertainty.

Think about the passage of your life until now. Hasn't it been like a movie? Think about some of your most tragic, magic, comic, sad, happy experiences.

Wouldn't they have made great movie scripts? How many times have you watched M-Net or the big screen and felt a sense of *déjà vu*, a sense of having played the role that the actors are playing? That is why movies are so powerful. They are dramatic projections of our own lives. Now think of the last suspense movie or thriller you have watched. You spent the time in a state of tension and uncertainty. Was the heroine going to make it or not? Would they live or would they die? Would he and she live happily ever after or wouldn't they?

It is one thing to experience suspense and tension vicariously through the celluloid images in front of you while you sit in the darkness munching your popcorn. You know that the Hollywood scriptwriter has probably written a happy ending because happy endings sell movies. It's an entirely different and more unpleasant matter to experience suspense, uncertainty and tension in your real life. What's more, if you experience inner uncertainty and tension, you involuntarily send out this signal to the people around you. The answer? Self-visualisation.

Self-visualisation is when you can actually see, touch, feel, taste and hear what it is going to be like to live your ABHAG. It is a kind of multi-sensory virtual experience in your head. ABHAG goes further than setting yourself a goal: it actually means living your goal in advance and becoming so certain that you will realise your ABHAG that you move beyond confidence into a new level of certainty. When you get into this state of certainty, other people feel it. You radiate this self-visualisation so powerfully that people and life become your allies in making your ABHAG happen. There is no scientific premise to explain how this happens. The force that will empower you is far greater than science. You just have to open yourself up to it.

Self-visualisation is a very simple process: it is called dreaming with your eyes open. Discard all limitations. We are talking about a dream here, a dream that nevertheless is achievable. *Try it now.*

☛ First, review your personal blueprint, because it leads to realising your ABHAG.

☛ Secondly, project yourself 18 months into the future.

☛ Thirdly, paint your picture of success. Think about what you desire to do the most 18 months from now and write down your answers. What position will you hold? What company will you be running or working for? What do you absolutely love doing? What really turns you on? What service will you be offering? What product will you be selling? What clients will you have? What will your monthly sales be? How much money will you be making? What image will people have of you? What emotions will you be feeling? Which achievement will you become famous for? What do you consider to be your ultimate achievement, the furthest you can possibly stretch yourself? (As you write down the answers to these self-visualisation questions, remember to make them as exciting and vivid as possible. Read the section on The Thoughts and Language of Success on page 109 again for help.)

☛ Fourthly, as you do with your personal blueprint, continually view your picture of success until it becomes as real to you as your immediate circumstances. Live with it until it becomes your constant mental companion, until it becomes instinct. It will become real. Take a leap of faith and really see yourself living it.

The process of self-visualisation begins with passion. The image in your mind must excite you; it must be something that you passionately want to achieve. As you move towards it, you get into the flow, the current starts carrying you as people and life propel you towards your destiny.

Nicola's dream: join the club…

To prove to you just how powerful and simple self-visualisation can be, we offer you the story of Nicola White. Nicola was the manager of a budget hotel in Cape Town. The hotel is part of a national chain and Nicola was becoming frustrated with her lack of progress. She had been a manager for three years and she believed she was capable of a lot more. (Remember: frustration is an exciting emotional signal.) We might add that Nicola was a tall, striking woman in her early thirties with great presence and a sharp wit.

Nicola attended one of Mike's seminars on self-visualisation because, although she felt she was capable of a lot more, she did not quite know what she really wanted to do. Mike asked Nicola what her self-visualisation was. She gave him the usual response: 'I don't know, I don't have one.' Mike probed further. 'I accept that,' he said, 'but if you did have a vision for yourself, what would it be? What would you like to do more than anything else?' Nicola thought for a few moments and then replied with total sincerity, 'I would like to run a really high-class nightclub and restaurant. I know I am good with people, I've proved I can handle pressure and long hours, I have extensive experience in the hospitality industry, I am a good business manager. In fact, my hotel has the best margins in the group. And my hobby is gourmet cooking. My friends are always asking me to help them prepare meals for their dinner parties.' This was the first time that Nicola had actually taken stock of her strengths, and it was the first time that she had actually focused on what her dream could be. It was fascinating to watch her as she became increasingly animated.

Mike asked her a few more questions. 'Nicola, what is this nightclub and restaurant going to look like? What kind of food are you going to serve? What kind of music are you going to play? What is going to set this restaurant and nightclub apart from all the other clubs and restaurants in the city?' Nicola thought a while before responding. 'Well,' she said slightly out of breath with excitement, 'the colours are going to be understated. Pastels, I think. And I'm going to have live jazz. We have so much talent in this city and no one seems to be developing it to its full potential. I'm going to serve good, wholesome, traditional English fare. No one can make a roast like me and you just cannot believe what I can do with vegetables. But you know what is really going to set my place apart? The whole place, even the bouncers, will be run by women — attractive, sexy, classy, smart women. What's more, we are all going to wear pin-stripe suits over black body stockings. And I'm going to call it Nicci's.' Nicola stopped suddenly, amazed at her own vision. Then, a split second later, the whole room erupted into applause. Everyone was inspired by her self-visualisation.

Nicola is well on her way to realising her dream. While she still has her job as the hotel manager, she has put together a business plan and an outline of her unique concept, which she is currently presenting to potential backers for start-up capital. Most importantly, Nicola feels more alive than she has in a long time. She has purpose and she has direction. Do you? Do you remember Barbara Heyburgh, Christine Searll and Solly Krynauw from the previous chapter? They all went through the same process to unleash their personal power.

Mike's Achievable Big Hairy Audacious Goal

Let Mike share his self-visualisation, and how it has helped him. 'My Achievable Big Hairy Audacious Goal is that in 18 months' time I am going to be performing in front of packed houses at prominent theatres around the country — the Civic in Johannesburg, the Baxter in Cape Town and the Playhouse in Durban. I am going to have a run of ten nights at each venue, and every night will be a sell-out. I know it will be a sell-out because I am going to get a major broadcaster and a national brand to sponsor the event and the advertising. What's more, *Fire & Water* will be so successful that people will want to come and hear me talk about it live. In just one month, I will reach approximately

30 000 people live. The show will also be financially lucrative, because the tickets will cost at least R100.

'The show will start at 8 p.m. and run until 11.30 p.m. with a 25-minute break for intermission. I will start the show off with my favourite song, "I Feel Good" by James Brown. Then, throughout the show, I'll play such classic rock and soul music as Steppenwolf, Aretha Franklin, George Benson, Ray Charles, The Rolling Stones, Tina Turner, Bruce Springsteen, Luther Vandross and others.

'I will be at my absolute best every night for 30 nights because I will be making my dream come true. By the end of each session, the audience will be so moved, motivated and emotional, that they will give me a standing ovation and shout "Viva, Lipkin, Viva!!"

'Can you see the scene I've just created for you? I'm sure you can. It's the end of my long-term movie. And you know what? In my mind, it has already happened. I'm in lag time now. I've played it so many times in my head that it has become part of my mental software. I have absolute certainty that it will happen.

'The most extraordinary consequence of my self-visualisation is the momentum that it gives me every day in my career as a motivational speaker. In 1996 alone, I have staged ten public events attracting close to 500 people at a time. And every single event is a dress rehearsal for my Achievable Big Hairy Audacious Goal.

'It has even helped me in my role as a talkshow host on Radio 702. Some time ago, I was scheduled to interview a leading businessperson as my guest on Power Talk. The show is on air from 6 p.m. to 7 p.m. I usually get to the studio by 5.40 p.m. My guests usually arrive by about 5.50 p.m. However, on this particular Sunday night, no guest arrived. Needless to say, I panicked. How could I have a talkshow if I didn't have a guest? I had tens of thousands of people waiting to listen to an interview that was not going to take place. As the news announcer read the 6 p.m. news, I was almost sick with worry and nervousness. I thought that this was the end of my career in broadcasting.

'Then, literally 60 seconds before I was due to go on air, I had a revelation, an exquisite mental breakthrough. I thought of my dream, and suddenly I switched from extreme panic to extreme excitement. "If your dream is to talk to 30 000 people live in a single month," I said to myself, "what do you think is about to happen now? You get to speak to 30 000 people live in a single night! You're a heartbeat away from making your dream come true. Although it's not face to face, it is ear to ear." The moment I saw my current reality within the context of my dream, I felt in control. I knew that what I had to do was to deliver a great solo motivational talk over the airwaves.

'Well, the show was so successful that 702 decided to extend my show by an extra hour so that I could have a solo show every week. My show is now from 5 p.m. to 7 p.m. every Sunday. The first hour, called The Hour of Power, is my motivational talk while the second hour is taken up by the guest interview.

'I'm telling you this because it is our self-visualisation that guides us during times of uncertainty or difficulty. If I didn't have my dream, I would never have been able to turn a potentially traumatic situation into the best thing that could have happened to me.'

Reg's Achievable Big Hairy Audacious Goal

Reg shares his Achievable Big Hairy Audacious Goal: 'It was always our dream at Hunt Lascaris TBWA to become the first world-class communications group out of Africa. In fact, it still is because however good we become, we can always be better. Everything we do is geared towards meeting and beating the world's best. We continually saw ourselves as world class and held ourselves to this higher standard. In 1993, however, our dream was realised when we were formally acknowledged as the International Advertising Agency of the Year by *Advertising Age*, the world's premier advertising and marketing journal. It was the first time any ad agency out of Africa had won the award. It would have been unthinkable for a South African company to be acknowledged in this fashion even a year before. However, because it is so easy to become complacent, achieving that goal could have become a liability. The day after the award was made, John Hunt and I communicated the following message to all our people: "But that was yesterday…"'

Walt saw it first

One of the great motivational stories on the power of self-visualisation comes from Walt Disney. Walt Disney had a great dream to develop the world's most captivating theme park in Orlando, Florida. He bought the land and designed the park right down to its finest detail. It was to be the crowning achievement of his awesome career. However, he died before the park became a reality. On the opening day, thousands of people streamed through the turnstiles, their faces eager with anticipation. As they watched the flow of people into the park, a local newsman said to Roy Disney, Walt's brother, 'What a pity Walt didn't live to see this day.' Roy replied, 'On the contrary, Walt saw it first. That's why you're seeing it now.'

What have you seen? What is your life's masterpiece? Begin sculpting it now!

The fifth principle of personal marketing:

The principle of self-rejuvenation

rejuvenate: to make young again; restore to youthful vigour
— Webster's Dictionary

No matter what our occupation, we are all in the fashion business. We are either hot or we're not. We are either relevant or irrelevant. We are either winning or losing. We are either fresh or we're stale. There is no middle path. We are either in or we're out. Where are you? Are you in fashion? Are you perceived as a winner? Are you at the forefront of whatever you are doing, or are you still saying and doing the same things you said or did yesterday? Are you surfing down the wave of the next trend, or are you in way over your head? What are you doing to constantly rejuvenate yourself physically, emotionally and mentally?

In a country as fluid as South Africa, the principle of self-rejuvenation determines how sharp or blunt our edge is. It determines our level of energy, vitality and creativity. However, this principle is continually overlooked in favour of urgent tasks that require immediate attention. Day by day, we run our batteries down. We deplete our resources. Fatigue sets in. Our joy of life deserts us and we head into the spiral of staleness, burnout and depression.

The principle of self-rejuvenation is not a luxury: it is an absolute necessity. Self-rejuvenation is the source of the other seven principles. The principle of self-rejuvenation is not just a practice, it is a state of mind. Whether you are an adman or an accountant, victory goes to those who keep renewing their sources of inspiration and creativity. The principle of self-rejuvenation demands that we keep filling up our personal reservoirs with the possibilities and promises of life. It means staying fresh all the time, because you never know when the breakthrough moment will present itself to you.

Contrary to conventional wisdom, luck is not a form of good fortune that comes to you like manna from heaven. Webster's Dictionary defines luck beautifully as 'the force that seems to operate for good or ill in a person's life, as in shaping circumstances, events, opportunities'. We, however, believe that you are in control of that force. To paraphrase that well-known line in 'Star Wars': you invite the force to be with you. The fine folks at Nando's understood this when they said in their core beliefs that *justice and good luck will only come to our aid if we always try to do the right thing, even when it is the most difficult thing.* Like attracts like, and great opportunities are drawn to those who keep their spirits and their minds fertile, vibrant and receptive to wonder.

During the 1996 BMW Innovative Thinking Conference held in Cape Town, John Kotter had this to say about the power of self-rejuvenation and the failure to apply it:

'Youth is not a time of life; it is a state of mind; it is not a matter of rosy cheeks, red lips and supple knees; it is a matter of the will, a quality of the imagination, a vigour of the emotions; it is the freshness of the deep springs of life. Youth means the temperamental predominance of courage over timidity, of the appetite for adventure over the love of ease. This often exists in a man of 60 more than in a boy of 20. Nobody grows old merely by a number of years. We grow old by deserting our ideals. Years may wrinkle the skin, but to give up enthusiasm wrinkles the soul. Worry, fear, self-distrust bows the heart and turns the spirit back to dust. Whether 60 or 16, there is in every human being's heart the lure of wonder, the unfailing childlike attitude of what's next, and the joy of the game of living. In the centre of your heart and my heart there is a radio station; so long as it receives messages of beauty, hope, cheer, courage and power from people and from the infinite, so long are you young. When the aerials are down, and your spirit is covered with snows of cynicism and the ice of pessimism, then you are grown old, even at 20; but as long as your aerials are up, to catch waves of optimism, there is hope you may die young at 80.'

The Tina Turner principle: self-rejuvenation to the power of ten

To prove the power of Kotter's words to ourselves, we looked at the volatile, fad-driven, brutal business of pop and rock music. We asked ourselves which artists really owned the minds of the millions of young music fans. We were amazed to discover that the most popular and powerful music masters are in their mid to late forties, fifties and even sixties — Mick Jagger and the Rolling Stones, Elton John, Billy Joel, Paul McCartney, Phil Collins, Bruce Springsteen,

Sting, ZZ Top, George Benson, James Brown, Ray Charles, and, of course, Tina Turner, the grand old dame of rock. The two of us attended her concert at Ellis Park in 1996. As we walked around the stadium in awe, we watched the thousands of teenagers and early 20-somethings dance, mesmerised by her spell. They were not thinking about her age, they were captivated by her youth, energy, passion and vigour. We all have a Tina Turner inside; we just have to let her out.

The Mandela factor: How to be responsibly outrageous

South Africa is the only country on earth where an almost 80-year-old man sets fashion trends. The 'Mandela shirt' has permeated South African fashion to the point where even the Olympic team's uniforms were influenced by his dress. At every cocktail party we attend, we see South Africa's new movers and shakers adorned in the loose, flowing, boldly patterned silk shirts inspired by Madiba.

Mandela's true personal marketing genius expressed itself when he stepped on to the Ellis Park rugby field for the 1995 Rugby World Cup final dressed in the number six Springbok rugby jersey, and when he stepped on to the soccer field in the African Nations Cup Final, again dressed in the captain's colours. Those two actions epitomise the entire spirit of this book. He showed us how to be responsibly outrageous; how to loosen up; how to rejuvenate both one-self and others by being bold, colourful and surprising. Mandela did it for the nation. Whom can you do it for? When was the last time that you did some-thing responsibly outrageous to rejuvenate your company, your department, your team, your family, your friends, your colleagues? Let go of those inhibi-tions or outmoded rules of conduct that inhibit you. No matter your age, be loose, be young, be free.

That is why the two of us are so optimistic about the future of this country and its people. We are losing our inhibitions. We are saying and doing things that would have been unthinkable — or even punishable by law — in the old South Africa. Can you imagine a John Vorster, a PW Botha or a CJ Swart don-ning a rugby jersey and striding smilingly and jauntily on to the field in full view of millions of people? Come to think of it, we cannot imagine any of them smiling at all.

50 ways of self-rejuvenation

In researching and writing this book, we spoke to hundreds of self-rejuvenating people from every slice of South African society to discover how they renew themselves. We would like to share their as well as some of our own insights and actions with you.

1. Eat passion fruit. Try mopane worms at least once.
2. Go into the bush as often as you can.
3. Take a walk on the wild side.
4. Get teenagers to teach you. They know everything.
5. Jump in puddles.
6. Invite someone dangerous to tea.
7. Read the *Sowetan*.
8. Watch pop videos.
9. Watch 'The Wizard of Oz' and 'Gone with the Wind' one more time.
10. Read at least one book a month. Any book.
11. Spend one hour looking at the sky, the grass, the flowers and the trees.
12. Every week, do something that you are afraid to do. Get the fear out of your life.
13. Laugh at anything, smile at everything.
14. Surf the Internet and enjoy the adult entertainment.
15. Hug someone.
16. Wear bright colours. Fluorescent is good.
17. Wear clothes that you feel good in and to hell with the critics.
18. Wear mint-flavoured condoms.
19. Sit around an open fire and toast marshmallows.
20. Never feel sorry for yourself. It doesn't help.
21. Find something to praise yourself for, stroke your own hair and say: 'I'm really proud of you.' Find the applause within.
22. If it is not your usual role, prepare a meal for your family or friends — an omelette, spaghetti, braaivleis, it doesn't matter.
23. Treat your partner to breakfast in bed on a tray with real linen at least once a year.
24. Buy a pack of wax crayons and draw a picture of your dream. Then hang it up where everyone can see it. If you need guidance, call any three-year-old.
25. Walk wherever possible, run if you can, and never hide.
26. Munch apples, suck oranges and drink carrot juice.
27. Eat chicken with your hands. Squeeze mielie pap before you pop it into your mouth.
28. Avoid lying — to anyone, and to yourself most of all.
29. Learn to speak a language other than English. Zulu or Xhosa would be good.

30. Reduce your debts. It helps you to breathe easier.
31. Skinny dip with someone you love.
32. Go body surfing.
33. Give your petrol attendant a R20 tip.
34. Trust everybody over and under 30, unless they give you good reason to do otherwise.
35. Stay away from haters and run away from negaholics.
36. Go to a driving range and hit balls, even if you don't play golf. Hit a punching bag, even if you don't box. Slice the air in powerful chops and shout Japanese affirmations at the top of your voice, even if you don't do karate.
37. Go on a picnic with fine friends and fine wine. Take a nap on the grass.
38. Do not kick dogs, cats, people or any other living creature.
39. Say 'please', 'thank you' and 'I love you', always.
40. Forgive everybody, including yourself, every night just before you go to sleep.
41. Since you cannot be someone else, be yourself and be your own hero.
42. Always keep a notebook and pen with you. Write down every great idea you get. Act on it. Great ideas are like fireflies in the night. You need to capture them immediately before they disappear.
43. Maintain a sense of adventure, even when you're meeting with your accountant.
44. Always have an answer to the question: 'What would I do if I lost my job tomorrow?'
45. Take the blame when it's your mistake; take the credit when it's due; celebrate opinions different to yours.
46. Don't whine.
47. When you're driving your car and another driver cuts you off, flashes his lights at you from behind, or jumps a red light, don't get angry. Tell yourself that his wife is in labour and he's on his way to attend the birth of his firstborn.
48. When you're on a roll and everything clicks for you, take maximum advantage. When the opposite is true, hold steady and wait it out.
49. Learn how to be a great teamplayer; but never invite someone on to your team who you wouldn't trust with your kids.
50. It's okay to be crazy. In fact, you have to be crazy to stay sane in South Africa. Sanity is merely the playground for the unimaginative.

Feeling rejuvenated, revved up and ready to go? The next principle awaits.

The sixth principle of personal marketing:

The principle of reciprocation — do unto others...

reciprocation: given or felt by each towards the other; to give or feel in return; a mutual giving and receiving

— WEBSTER'S DICTIONARY

If there is one defining trait of a South African management style, it is the pre-disposition to catch people doing things wrong. We come from the heavy-handed school of management: almost all stick and no carrot. Apartheid has conditioned us to look for the differences between people, not the common ground. We viewed each other with suspicion. Trust has become the rarest commodity of all. Our way is always the right way. Have you ever noticed how anyone who doesn't agree with you is not only wrong but an idiot as well? The best definition of justice the two of us have heard? When you get your own way...

Go for the magic in the other person

The word 'magic' has been used 24 times in this book. But do you know what it really means? Webster's Dictionary defines magic as 'an irresistible or extra-ordinary charm, influence or power'. If you look carefully and lovingly enough, you will find this power in everyone you meet. Most of us, though, zoom in on the negatives we can find in the other person. The main differ-ence between humans and God is that God doesn't presume to judge us until the end of our days. Humans judge one another on impact. Think about your own response to people you have just met. Unless you are Desmond Tutu, you probably make an instant decision on the other person's character. Have you ever noticed how we judge other people by their behaviour while judging ourselves by our intentions — which are always perfect, of course?

How do you feel when you are with someone who is looking for the negatives in you? How do you feel when the other person signals suspicion, hostility or disapproval through tone of voice or physiology? What happens to your personal energy in such cases? Think about the rising tension that fills the space between you. Think about your levels of motivation to go above and beyond for this person. Now think about how you feel when you are with someone who looks for the magic in you. Think about the last time that you were with a person who wanted to believe in you; who was prepared to give you the benefit of the doubt; who signalled their desire to help or develop you; who caught you doing something right and praised you for it; who signalled through their tone of voice and physiology that they liked you.

We feel empowered and inspired when we are with people who show that they enjoy being with us. We feel depleted and drained when we are with people who show that they do not like us or are looking to catch us out and prove us wrong. Mike experiences this response every time he speaks to an audience. Where an audience is suspicious of Mike, or when they believe that Mike is out to manipulate them, or where there is tension in the company and people see Mike as a political ploy, Mike knows that it is going to be an incredibly hard session. It is like swimming against the emotional current. He usually knows that it is going to be rough within the first few seconds of the talk or workshop.

On the other hand, when Mike is confronted by a highly receptive audience, an audience that shows that they are delighted to have the opportunity to listen to him, Mike's passion is fired up and he plays at the top of his game. He returns their affection with a stunning performance.

That is the principle of reciprocation: *if you overtly express your affection and respect for others, it is almost impossible for them not to like and respect you. If you express your dislike and disrespect for others in any way, it is impossible for them to like and respect you.*

The principle of reciprocation is your prize for observing the golden rule of doing unto others as you would have them do unto you. It can also be your penalty for failing to do so. It is the most important personal marketing principle for developing and sustaining great relationships. Rapport is the essence of mutually rewarding and enduring relationships. Rapport is harmonious relations; it is when you feel emotionally nourished by the other person; it is when you feel as though they understand you, respect you, like you and share your values. We all want to be with people who like us, who are like us or people who are how we would like to be. Rapport is found in the common ground between people, not in the dissimilarities. Do you ever say: 'I like that person because we've got big differences', or do you say: 'I like that person because we've got so much in common'?

People who have mastered the principle of reciprocation are masters at relationship-building. They have the ability to generate instant rapport by broadcasting their affection and respect for the other person in an open and ongoing manner. The two of us make a living by applying the principle of reciprocation. We interact with a diverse range of people from South Africa and the rest of the world on a daily basis. Our success rests on our capacity to connect immediately with people and then to sustain that connection over time. Let's share with you the specific ways in which we apply the principle of reciprocation for maximum impact:

☞ When you meet a person for the first time or when you are having a passing conversation with a stranger, demonstrate your affection for them via your smile, your handshake, your words and your tone of voice. Remember: be kind to strangers because you never know when you are entertaining an angel.

☞ You need empathy. Empathy is the ability to vicariously experience or accurately identify with the feelings, thoughts or attitudes of others. It is the highest form of listening, because when you are empathising, you are not just listening to what is being said, you are also listening to the way in which it is being said and you are listening for the real reason why it is being said. You cannot have empathy with someone else unless you genuinely care for them. It is only this sincere interest in the other person that develops your social antennae. Empathy is when you have cleared your mind and are concentrating single-mindedly on connecting with the other person.

Listen to how people say what they say. Observe their physiology: are they bored, irritated, interested, motivated, fearful, trusting, suspicious, friendly, or hostile? The words we use are only seven per cent of all communication. The other 93 per cent is non-verbal communication. How things are said is 38 per cent of communication, while our physiology and physical appearance are 55 per cent of communication.

☞ Make it a conscious habit to actively look for the magic and the good in the other person. Focus on finding the best part of them, even when they are showing you the worst part of them.

☞ Adopt their way of speaking and posture. Lower your voice when you are talking to a softspoken person. Mirror their physiology. Get into their rhythm and on to their frequency. Don't expect them to get on to yours.

☞ Listen to the words they use and weave their words into your speech.

When Mike speaks to the guys at Nando's, he uses these words: 'You guys are really hot. You guys are sizzling. I hope you guys have an appetite for something delicious this afternoon because I have an idea that will make your mouth water.'

When Mike speaks to a bank or financial services company, he says, 'We need to improve our relationships with our clients by depositing more into the emotional bank account. Currently we may be withdrawing more than we can afford to. In fact, we are in emotional bank account overdraft. We need to invest more in our clients because they are our most valuable, income-generating assets. What's more, if you hire me, I'll give you the highest return on your investment. And that's the bottom line.'

When he speaks to an automotive company, he says, 'We need to over-haul our marketing campaign because we are not firing on all cylinders. This engine needs to be tuned because this is where the rubber hits the road. We need to recharge our batteries and put the pedal to the metal.'

Recently, Mike was manipulated into doing someone a favour because the principle of reciprocation was applied to him. A woman from Cape Town named Karen called to ask Mike for free advice on how to market a new service she was considering launching. Mike was extremely busy, and he looked for an excuse to turn her down. Before he could speak, she said to him, 'I just want to tap into your energy for a couple of hours.' It just so happens that 'tapping into your energy' is one of Mike's favourite phrases. So what went through his mind when he heard Karen say that she just wanted to tap into his energy? Answer: 'Karen shares my values and view of life. I want to meet her.' Mike agreed to help her. What Mike didn't know at the time was that Karen and he had a mutual friend who is also a motivational speaker and who has attended the same programmes as Mike. The mutual friend told Karen that if she told Mike that she wanted to 'tap into his energy' Mike would do anything for her. Mike fell for it hook, line and sinker.

Make every effort to understand, respect and reflect the culture and style of the people you are dealing with. That is why it is so important to learn the language of the majority of South Africans. Even if you have just a basic knowledge, if you can only greet them in their language, it will make a huge difference to your relationships with people.

You want the other person to say about you, 'Hey, I like that guy/girl because they're just like me. They share my values. They understand what I'm all about and they talk my language. I feel comfortable with him/her. I'd like to spend more time with him/her.'

☛ Go out of your way to compliment the other person. Catch them doing something right. Don't be shy. Think about how great you feel when someone says to you, 'I think you're fantastic,' or 'I thought you were great,' or 'I really appreciated it when you did that for me,' or 'It's great to be on your team.' One small warning, though: don't overdo it. Do not engage in meaningless flattery. Be sincere.

How often do you use the word 'sincere'? How many times have you signed your letters, 'Yours sincerely'? Do you know what it means? It actually means 'without wax'. In Roman times, when a marble merchant attempted to sell an inferior, flawed piece of marble, he would fill the cracks and flaws with wax. However, the superior quality pieces didn't need this measure of deceit. When you sign your letters 'Yours sincerely', you are promising the recipient that you are being totally honest and genuine and that you are giving them a superior quality product, service or performance. Before you sign your next letter 'without wax', make sure that you can deliver on that promise.

Romance those who have already given you their love and loyalty

It is extraordinary that we reserve the best parts of ourself for people we hardly know or have just met. The people closest to us get the tired, humdrum version of ourselves. Do you continually romance those who have already given you their love and loyalty, or do you slip into an unimaginative routine with your closest stakeholders?

Why do relationships wear away? Why do clients leave service providers with whom they've had long relationships? In the vast majority of cases, it is because the courtship ceases at some point and the drudgery begins. The best definition of a great lover that we have read comes from the writer Daphne du Maurier. She wrote, 'A great lover is not someone who has a different partner every night, it's someone who makes the same partner feel like a different partner every night.' This piece of social advice is not limited to your noctur-nal activities. It's the way to sustain healthy, vibrant, positively reciprocal rela-tionships. Variety is what adds *vooma* to your relationships.

Pauline's story

This is something that happened to Mike in the thriving metropolis of Welkom in early 1996. He was invited there to deliver a workshop with the Welkom Executive Secretaries' Club. Mike wanted to demonstrate that the more things change, the more they stay the same. He read the audience this excerpt from an annual financial report of the South African Breweries and asked the audience to guess when it was written: 'In presenting this report of the South African Breweries, the directors feel that, notwithstanding the troubled times passed through, the results of the year's trading are very satis-factory… The sales in Johannesburg during the past year would have been larg-er but for the interference with trade from political troubles during some of the best months.'

This is an excerpt from the first ordinary general meeting of SAB held at Winchester House, Old Broad Street, London, on 2 July 1896. So what has changed over the past 100 years? Mike then made a comment that trying to live life during the Anglo-Boer War must have been far more traumatic than life in South Africa in the 1990s. He then told this fateful joke. During the Anglo-Boer War, the British officers wore scarlet uniforms so that, when they were shot, their men couldn't see that they were bleeding. Which makes you wonder: why did the Boers wear khaki?

The room erupted into laughter, just as we're sure you're laughing now. Except for one woman. Her name was Pauline van Zyl. Mike knew her name was Pauline van Zyl because she was wearing a name tag that said: Pauline van Zyl. Pauline stood up, literally shaking with rage. Through clenched teeth, she hissed at Mike, 'That's not funny. My great-grandfather died in the Anglo-Boer War and my great-grandmother suffered terrible hardship in the concentra-tion camps. And you have the arrogance and insensitivity to mock their sac-rifice! Furthermore, you don't even know your history. The Boers did not wear khaki. They went to battle in the clothes that they wore at home.'

The room went very quiet. A hundred pairs of eyes turned to Mike to see how he would handle the situation. Ask yourself how you would have han-dled the situation. Every day, we find ourselves in situations where something we have said unwittingly angers somebody else.

Armed with the principle of reciprocation, Mike's response was, 'Pauline, I'm terribly sorry. If I had known that your great-grandparents paid such a terrible price, I would never have told the joke. It was wrong of me. If my family had suffered like yours, I would have reacted exactly the way you did. I admire you very much for standing up for what you believe in. It took a lot of guts to do what you just did in front of a hundred other people.' Mike smiled at her, walked over to Pauline and embraced her. The transformation was miraculous. Pauline's eyes moistened as she returned the embrace. Throughout the rest of the evening she listened riveted to Mike's words. At the end of the workshop, she even bought his book *Lost and Found*. Although it was just a little incident, Mike regards Pauline's turnaround as one of his finest achievements. Let's examine the elements that Mike used to turn Pauline around:

☛ Firstly, Mike admitted that he was wrong.
☛ Secondly, he demonstrated his empathy with Pauline's feelings.
☛ Thirdly, he focused on the magic in her. He found a reason to praise her action in a sincere way.
☛ Fourthly, he lived his personal blueprint by physically demonstrating his affection for Pauline through a hug.

God lives in the little things

Pauline's story is a little episode in the greater scheme of things. But it taught us the importance of treating every human being we meet with affection and respect. Life is tough, times are tough, business is tough. And tough times call for tough measures. However, we believe that courtesy, kindness and the principle of reciprocation are the hallmarks of great relationship-builders. The demonstration of humanity, caring, appreciation and recognition is manifested in the little things we do every day. But then God lives in the little things. *Woza Moya.*

The seventh principle of personal marketing:
The principle of contribution — always give more than you take

'The secret to living is giving. All that is not given is lost. Service is the rent we pay for living here.'

— MAHATMA GANDHI

The essence of the principle of contribution is: if you want to achieve what you want to achieve, help other people to achieve what they want to achieve.

The universal law of relationships is that if you always give more than you take, you always receive more than you expect. The people who ultimately thrive in the game called life are those people who contribute to the quality of life of the people around them. They understand that people want to be with, work with, live with, and buy from people who have a *mutuality of interest* with them. Mutuality of interest means that you consider the other person's interests as important as your own. It means that you are a coach and a mentor of others, because you know that the only way you can grow and stretch is by helping others to grow and stretch.

How do you feel when you come face to face with a salesperson or service provider who looks at you as though you are nothing more than next month's bond payment? How do you feel when you go into a clothing store and the attendant tells you that the outfit you tried on was made for you, even though it makes you look like Godzilla? How do you feel when you are confronted by people who see you merely as a vehicle for their own gratification? Repulsed, revolted, resentful and resistant? That kind of person has zero influence.

Their personal marketing power is minimised by their own selfishness. They are devoid of mutuality of interest.

Don't get us wrong here. We are not Father Teresa. We are motivated by the profit principle. However, money is not our prime motivator. Money is a yardstick of our performance. Remember the biblical warning: not money, but 'the love of money is the root of all evil'. If you are motivated solely by personal gain, you will screw up. You can fool some of the people all of the time and all of the people some of the time, but not all the people all the time. The moment you become branded as a non-contributor, you become history. People will shun you. And you can take that prediction to the bank.

In his book *Lost and Found*, Mike invited readers to verbalise their fears, challenges and personal situations by writing to him under guaranteed confidentiality. More than half of the hundreds of letters he received were from people in a state of extreme anxiety or depression that was caused by loss of money or material possessions. In almost all of these cases, there was no awareness of the need for contribution whatsoever. Somehow, many people believe that the pursuit of money or material possessions is a worthy life's mission. Their entire view of the world and their role in it revolves around this perception. When their money or material possessions are taken away from them, they feel as though part of themselves has been amputated.

When you give, you are restoring in yourself that force that makes you human

Heed the ancient biblical injunction to give a tithe. Most people respond to this notice with the comment, 'I can't. I'm already giving 45 per cent to the taxman.' We are not talking about money only here. We are talking about time and effort. We are blinded by our self-interest, because when we give to others we are really making a down payment on our future and the future of all our personal stakeholders. The principle of contribution means taking a longer-term view. It means delaying the immediate gratification that may result from only pursuing your own goals. It is the difference between spending your capital now and investing it in a highly lucrative endowment policy. We believe that life is really a series of deposits and withdrawals in relationships. Every time that you contribute towards a relationship, you increase not only your equity with the other person but also the interest that equity generates. We all need our own private RDP.

Look around you. Think of the truly successful people, people who have sustained success over the long haul. We guarantee you that they are all contributors to life and to other people. Think of those people who keep losing it: aren't they the kind of people who fail to observe this principle?

Give before you have to give. Live the truest cliché we know: it's better to give than to receive. Take stock right now. Think about whether you have been giving more than you have been receiving. When you have given, was it done grudgingly? Mandise Williams, head of the Red Cross in South Africa, made these poignant remarks to Mike on Power Talk: 'To you, it may just be a little thing, but to someone else, your small act of contribution means a great deal… I think that giving helps you stay vigilant against the lure of complacency… What I believe very strongly is that when you give, you have to give with respect, so that the dignity of the recipient, which is already depleted by their situation, gets nurtured… When you give, you are restoring in yourself that force that makes you human… We dare not look down upon those who have fallen on hard times because there but for the grace of God go us all… It is a privilege to give simply because you are in a position to do so.'

Contribution is more powerful than Prozac in fighting depression

The 21 July 1996 edition of the *Sunday Independent* newspaper quotes Dr Dot Siwinska, a psychiatrist running a private practice, as saying, 'There is a depression epidemic in Gauteng.' (By the way, Gauteng is really South African for Gotham.) More and more, South Africa is becoming a Prozac nation. Dr Mark Nathan, a British registrar in psychiatry based at Baragwanath Hospital is quoted in the same article as saying, 'Prozac is dispensed all the time at Baragwanath. But let's face it, even the best antidepressants are still horse pills. Psychiatry is where medicine was 30 years ago.'

Nathan goes on to make an amazing comparison between South Africa and his native country. 'Practising psychiatry at Baragwanath often yields far more positive results than in England. I think a significant reason for this is that the extended family support system, with its built-in ethos of "help your neighbour", is still pretty strong among black people here. Most of my patients are discharged to some kind of family setting where there is great tolerance of mental disorder compared with England's arm's-length society. Practising as a state psychiatrist in London, you're basically just mopping up the debris of an alienated nation.' It seems as though the spirit of *ubuntu* is mightier than the drug.

At least ten to 15 per cent of all South African adults will experience a severe depression during their lifetime. A lot more of us, however, will experience prolonged periods of low-grade depression. This is where we manage to cope on a day-to-day basis but where the flavour has gone out of our life.

In this state, we do just enough to survive, and we certainly do nothing to market ourselves to others. In fact, the longer you stay in this state, the more you depreciate your personal brand value. Do you know what the most powerful remedy for depression is? Contribution. In all the literature on depression, the act of helping others even worse off than yourself has been shown to be the most powerful way of restoring your lust for life. It also is the least common phenomenon. So start giving and start living — and share this message with everyone you meet.

There is no limit to the amount of energy or love you can give

energy: capacity for vigorous activity; available power
— WEBSTER'S DICTIONARY

The performance of any human being at any stage is directly related to the amount of energy they have at the time. However, while the prime source of our raw physical energy may be the food we eat, the prime source of our emotional and psychic energy is other people. We have already spoken about how contagious our moods and emotions are. You become the company that you keep. Let's share the ultimate secret of personal effectiveness with you: *There is no limit to the amount of energy and love you can give. The more energy and love you give, the more you have to give. Energy and love are self-replenishing resources.*

Think of the high-energy, exceptionally loving people whom you know. Do you ever ask yourself how they sustain that level of intensity; how they never seem to go flat; how they stay so loving when so much horror is happening around them and even to them? Well, they have discovered, either consciously or unconsciously, that being in a state of energy and love is a much better place than feeling depleted and resentful. They have also discovered, consciously or unconsciously, that energy and love are two resources that expand when they are used. Once they had discovered that truth, they made the decision, again consciously or unconsciously, to keep using their energy and love.

If we asked you to run the Comrades Marathon tomorrow, could you? Well, unless you are among the 0,0003 per cent of the South African population who do run the event, the answer would probably be no. Why? Because you haven't trained to run it. Your muscles probably start hurting at the mere thought of it. Developing your love and energy muscles is much easier, but it takes discipline and exercise. You need to consciously decide to give as much love and energy as you can to everybody you meet, even strangers. Remember: there are no strangers, only friends we haven't met yet.

You need to continue giving energy and love to people even when this is not reciprocated. This is not altruism, charity or pure goodwill. Although the effect your love and energy will have on other people will be enormously motivating, the motive is a selfish one. Mike explains, 'I make a living from giving people energy and love. In fact, I am paid to energise people. But my main motivation is the way I feel while I do it. In my own mind, I have associated massive pleasure with giving people energy. I love it when I sense the spark in their eyes, the smile on their faces, the strut in their step, the warmth in their voice. So, because I want to pursue pleasure, I want to give more and more energy. The more I give the more I have to give. It's a positive, upward spiral. At the end of an eight-hour motivation session, I am often more energised than I was at the beginning. Many people, however, associate the giving of energy to others with hard work. They see it as a gruelling activity. They therefore shy away from doing it.'

When Dame Kiri Te Kanawa, the well-known New Zealand opera singer, was asked how she felt about having to go out every night and thrill thousands of people with her strenuous performances, she answered, 'I don't *have* to do anything; I *want* to.' Her answer sums up the spirit required to be a giver of energy.

Human beings are not camels. We can't store energy in the way that camels store water. You don't conserve energy by staying still. Energy is created by motion. Love is created by the act of loving. So become a lover right now! You'll love the way it makes you feel.

The eighth principle of personal marketing:
The principle of humour — go for the smile

humour: the faculty of perceiving what is amusing or comical; the faculty of expressing the amusing or comical

— WEBSTER'S DICTIONARY

During an expedition into the wildest part of darkest Africa, a group of explorers came upon a village of primitive savages. In an attempt to make friends of this very, very tough audience, who were watching the explorers' every move, the leader of the group tried to tell the natives what it was like in the civilised outside world. 'Out there,' he said, 'we love our fellow men.' The natives gave a ringing cry of 'Huzzanga!' to this. Encouraged by this the explorer continued, 'We treat others as we would want them to treat us.' 'Huzzanga!!' shouted the natives with much enthusiasm. 'We are peaceful,' said the explorer. 'Huzzanga!' cried the natives. With a tear running down his cheek, the explorer ended his fine speech, 'We come to you as friends, as brothers. So trust us. Open your arms to us, your homes, your hearts. What do you say?' The air shook with one mighty 'Huzzanga!!!' Greatly pleased by the reception, the leader of the explorers then began talking with the native's chief. 'I see you have cattle here,' he said. 'They are a species with which I am not familiar. May I inspect them?' 'Certainly, certainly, come right this way,' answered the chief. 'But be very careful as you walk that you do not step in the huzzanga.'

Are you smiling or even laughing? Humour is the magic potion for the human spirit. Laughter lightens moods; it relieves tension; it allows you to relate to any situation with a clearer perspective; it allows you to build an immediate emotional bond with other people. It also enhances your mental and physical state. How do you feel after a great laugh? Isn't it the second-best feeling you have ever had (and a lot safer)? The mere act of laughing releases a form of natural 'uppers' into the brain. Mike tells all the audiences that he addresses, 'We are all walking chemists. We can make our own drugs any time we want to. Simply by laughing, we can make ourselves feel better.' You need not sniff or smoke anything to get high — just laugh!

It is impossible not to like someone who has just made you smile or laugh. The person who can apply the deft touch of *appropriate* humour to any situation is the person who controls the climate of the situation. However, note the dictionary definition of humour: 'the ability to perceive the comic side of any situation before you can express the comedy in the situation'.

Are you the kind of person who is constantly looking for the lighter side of every situation? Do you go for the smile, or do you take yourself and life too seriously? If we have learnt one thing about mastering life, it is that we should never take ourselves too seriously. Whenever you do so, you misdirect and mismanage your passion so it turns on you, burns you and eventually destroys you. Angels understand this. That's why they can fly. They take themselves lightly.

Look at the people around you. People who manage their pressures well are also the people who are biased towards smiling, the people who manage to laugh their way through the turmoil, the people who help others see the funny side of not-so-funny things. Has anybody ever told you not to worry about this problem, you'll laugh about it later? Why wait? Laugh about it now! We have a simple philosophy that can be expressed in the following somewhat technical phrase: *Lag vir die kak!* (Laugh at the shit). And if you can't laugh about it because you haven't had enough practice yet, at least learn to smile.

Have you noticed that when someone near you yawns, you have a tendency to yawn in sympathy? It is the same with a smile. As long as we are not suspicious of their motives, we usually smile back at people who smile at us. The problem with most of us, however, is that when we are happy we don't tell our faces about it. The mere act of smiling can improve your mood. You are far more likely to feel good when you are smiling than when you are frowning. Try it now. Smile, then frown. You'll experience an instant mood swing.

Look at yourself in the mirror. Are you more attractive smiling or frowning? Are you more drawn to the face in the mirror when it appears happy or when it appears sad? Remember: other people can only judge what is going on inside of us by what they see on the outside of us. We respond instinctively to a smile — so practise smiling even when you are not entirely happy inside. Eventually we become what we do. If you smile, you will attract the goodwill of others, and that will go a long way towards helping you be happy.

The essence of personal marketing is the ability to differentiate ourselves from other people. Being a good personal marketer means being able to stand out from the crowd. A smile is the easiest, simplest and most rewarding way to achieve that. We told you that this book is all about simple ways to enhance your personal effectiveness. Look around you. How many people smile consistently in this pressure cooker of a country? A very small percentage, especially when the heat's on.

One warning about humour, however: it must be appropriate to the situation, people and cultures at hand. Nothing is worse than humour that either offends people or leaves them cold. The principle of humour requires sensitivity, empathy and timing. If you always honour and respect the people around you, the chances are you won't offend them.

Humour is a *learned skill*. Start practising the application of humour with people you know. Try it on your family and friends to begin with. Even if your humour bombs initially, they'll still love you. If you want to accelerate your learning of this vital skill, listen to or watch guys like Woody Allen or Robin Williams in action, or observe the people you know with a great sense of humour. Then develop your own brand of humour. You'll be so glad you did.

Epilogue
Practise focus, and focus on practice

Well, that's it, folks. We hope we've delivered on our promise to infotain you, that is, to inform and entertain you simultaneously.

We hope that you are equipped with at least one insight that you may not have had when you started this book.

We hope that we have inspired you with some of its stories, made you smile and sensitised you to those things you know you should be doing. Please write to us and tell us whether you think we have achieved our objectives. Once again, the address is *Fire & Water*, PO Box 41882, Craighall 2024.

The two most important words in our vocabulary are practise and focus. We practise focus and we focus on practice every day. True peak performance comes from doing something so often and so well that it becomes almost an instinct. It also comes from continually taking yourself to the next level, which is why we can never allow ourselves to slip into the deadly routine of time-worn habits.

Focus on what makes you strong, powerful, passionate and compassionate. You become your focus.

Treat the world as your laboratory: experiment, experiment, experiment.

Use your fear. It will serve you.

Ask your higher power to guide you. Trust your intuition, it's God's voice.

We thank you for sharing your time with us. And, until we meet again, live with passion!!

Imagination

edited by Rhodri Jones

H·E·B

Heinemann Educational Books
London

Heinemann Educational Books Ltd
LONDON EDINBURGH MELBOURNE AUCKLAND
TORONTO SINGAPORE HONG KONG KUALA LUMPUR
IBADAN NAIROBI JOHANNESBURG
NEW DELHI

ISBN 0 435 14481 2

Selection and arrangement © Rhodri Jones 1969
First published 1969
Reprinted 1970, 1972, 1974

Published by Heinemann Educational Books Ltd
48 Charles Street, London W1X 8AH
Printed Offset Litho in Great Britain by
Cox & Wyman Ltd, London, Fakenham and Reading

Acknowledgements

The Editor and Publisher wish to thank the following for permission to reprint copyright material: The Hogarth Press and the Literary Estate of Humbert Wolfe for 'The House of Ghosts'; Frances Cornford and The Cresset Press for 'Bickers Cottage' from *Collected Poems;* Laurence Lerner and Chatto & Windus Ltd for 'No Room for Ghosts' from *Directions of Memory;* Mrs George Bambridge and Macmillan & Co Ltd for 'The Way Through the Woods' from *The Collected Poems of Rudyard Kipling;* Robert Graves and Cassell & Co Ltd for 'Dicky', 'Welsh Incident', 'The Alice Jean', 'Lollocks', 'Last Love', and 'What did I dream?' from *Collected Poems 1965;* Guinness Superlatives Ltd and Alastair Thomson for 'The Lost Wolf' from *The Guinness Book of Poetry No 4;* Thomas Hennell and Oxford University Press for 'A Mermaiden' from *Poems;* permission to include 'Is my team ploughing?' has been granted by the Society of Authors as the literary representative of the Estate of A. E. Housman, and Jonathan Cape Ltd, publishers of A. E. Housman's *Collected Poems;* Mr Harold Owen and Chatto & Windus Ltd for 'Strange Meeting', 'Asleep', 'Conscious', and 'Mental Cases' from *Collected Poems;* Elizabeth Jennings and Andre Deutsch Ltd for 'Lazarus' and 'The Nightmare' from *Recoveries;* Thom Gunn and Faber & Faber Ltd for 'St. Martin and the Beggar' from *The Sense of Movement;* Peter Redgrove and Routledge & Kegan Paul Ltd for part of 'Conversation' from *The Nature of Cold Weather;* W. R. Rodgers and Secker & Warburg Ltd for 'The Internal Refugee' from *Awake and Other Poems;* Vernon Scannell for 'Banshee' and 'Gunpowder Plot' from *A Sense of Danger;* George Allen & Unwin Ltd for 'The Sentry' by Alun Lewis from *Raider's Dawn;* Faber & Faber Ltd for 'The Bat' and 'Night Crow' by Theodore Roethke from *Collected Poems;* permission to reproduce 'Solitude', 'The Owl', 'Drugged', and 'The Magnifying Glass' has been granted by the Literary Trustees of Walter de la Mare and the Society of Authors as their representative; Mrs Myfanwy Thomas and Faber & Faber Ltd for 'The Owl' and 'Cockcrow' from *Collected Poems of Edward Thomas;* Laurie Lee and Messrs Andre Deutsch Ltd for 'Town Owl' from *My Many-Coated Man;* Phoebe Hesketh and Rupert Hart-Davis Ltd for 'Fear by Moonlight' from *Prayer for Sun;* Ted Hughes and Faber & Faber Ltd for 'Insomniac' and 'Mushrooms' from *The Colossus and Other Poems;* Calder & Boyars Ltd for 'The Sleepwalker' from *Anthology of Modern Yugoslav Poetry;* B. S. Johnson and Constable & Co Ltd for

'Rejectamenta' from *Poems;* Max Harris and Angus & Robertson for 'The Tantanoola Tiger' from *Poetry in Australia;* Richard Wilbur and Faber & Faber Ltd for 'Digging for China' from *Poems 1943-1956;* Mrs Iris Wise and Macmillan & Co Ltd for 'The Shell' from *Collected Poems* by James Stephens; Charles Causley and Rupert Hart-Davis Ltd for 'Healing a Lunatic Boy'; Herbert Read and Faber & Faber Ltd for 'The Scene of War: Fear' from *Collected Poems;* Andrew Young and Ruper Hart-Davis Ltd for 'The Fear' from *Collected Poems;* Jon Stallworthy and Oxford University Press for 'The Trap' from *Out of Bounds;* Allen Tate and Eyre & Spottiswoode Ltd for 'The Wolves' from *Poems 1920-45;* George MacBeth and Scorpion Press for 'Bed-time Story' from *The Broken Places;* John Lehmann and William Heinemann Ltd for 'To Penetrate that Room' from *A Garden Revisited;* Gillian Pursey for 'The Witch'; Gillian Anderson for 'Fear'; George Sassoon and Faber & Faber Ltd for 'Enemies', 'Falling Asleep', 'Suicide in the Trenches' and 'Haunted' by Siegfried Sassoon in *Collected Poems;* Cobden-Sanderson for 'The Ocean in London' by Harold Munro in *Collected Poems;* Mrs John Freeman for 'To End Her Fear' by John Freeman; Mr Michael Gibson and Macmillan & Co Ltd for 'The Unseen Housemate'; The Trustees of the Hardy Estate and Macmillan & Co Ltd for 'The Choirmaster's Burial' and 'Something Tapped' by Thomas Hardy in *Collected Poems;* Peter Bland for 'The Nightwatchmen'.

Contents

Wonders and Terrors of the Mind

Supernatural

The House of Ghosts

Humbert Wolfe

First to describe the house. Who has not seen it
    once at the end of an evening's walk – the leaves
that suddenly open, and as sudden screen it
    with the first flickering hint of shadowy eaves?

Was there a light in the high window? Or
    only the moon's cool candle palely lit?
Was there a pathway leading to the door?
    Or only grass and none to walk on it?

And surely someone cried, 'Who goes there – who?'
    And ere the lips could shape the whispered 'I',
the same voice rose, and chuckled, 'You, 'tis you!'
    A voice, or the furred night-owl's human cry?

Who has not seen the house? Who has not started
    towards the gate half-seen, and paused, half-fearing
and half beyond all fear – and the leaves parted
    again, and there was nothing in the clearing?

The Haunted House

Thomas Hood

Unhinged the iron gates half open hung,
Jarred by the gusty gales of many winters,
That from its crumbled pedestal had flung
One marble globe in splinters.

No dog was at the threshold, great or small;
No pigeon on the roof – no household creature –
No cat demurely dozing on the wall –
Not one domestic feature.

No human figure stirred, to go or come,
No face looked forth from shut or open casement;
No chimney smoked – there was no sign of Home
From parapet to basement.

3

itch. By courtesy of John Hillelson Agency Ltd.

With shattered panes the grassy court was stirred;
The time-worn coping stone had tumbled after;
And thro' the ragged roof the sky shone, barred
With naked beam and rafter.

The flower grew wild and rankly as the weed,
Roses with thistles struggled for espial,
And vagrant plants of parasitic breed
Had overgrown the Dial.

The vine unpruned and the neglected peach,
Drooped from the wall with which they used to grapple;
And on the cankered tree, in easy reach,
Rotted the golden apple.

The pear and quince lay squandered on the grass;
The mould was purple with unheeded showers
Of bloomy plums – a Wilderness it was
Of fruits and weeds and flowers.

The very yew Formality had trained
To such a rigid pyramidal stature,
For want of trimming had almost regained
The raggedness of nature.

The Fountain was a-dry – neglect and time
Had marred the work of artisan and mason
And efts and croaking frogs, begot of slime
Sprawled in the ruined basin.

The Statue, fallen from its marble base,
Amidst the refuse leaves, and herbage rotten
Lay like the Idol of some bygone race,
Its name and rites forgotten.

On every side the aspect was the same,
All ruined, desolate, forlorn, and savage:
No hand or foot within the precinct came
To rectify or ravage.

For over all there hung a cloud of fear,
A sense of mystery the spirit daunted.
And said as plain as whisper in the ear,
The place is Haunted!

Bickers Cottage

Frances Cornford

Companionable ticking of the clock;
Collapsing of the coal;
The chair-legs warm;
Tobacco in a bowl;
The door sealed up;
The sooted kettle's hiss;
The firelit loaf; the cocoa-tin; the cup;
Outside the unplumbed night and pattering storm.

At such an hour as this
A ghost might knock,
Lacking unearthly comfort in its soul.

The Unseen Housemate

Wilfrid Gibson

A shuffling step across the upper floor,
Loose-fitting slippers flapping down the stair,
The handle turns and stealthily the door
Swings on its hinges, and there's no one there —
No one my eyes can see; but, happen, he
Who dwelt here ere I came had keener sight —
At least I wonder what he saw the night
He hanged himself from the old apple-tree.

No Room for Ghosts

Laurence Lerner

This house has no room for ghosts.
Neither periwigged gentlemen,
Spectres, nor skeletons
Clanging their scrap-iron
May tramp through the hall.
This house has no corners
For hiding the dead,

No cupboards nor passages, cellars or holes in the wall,
For the shadowy gentlemen
To step into, removing their head
As the landlady passes.
And the pale half-witted
Possibly murdered or even
Never existent uncle of whom we hear
Isn't welcome or even permitted
To re-appear.

This house is too full of noises,
Of children and cooking, arm-chairs, insistences, ructions,
Baked apples and broken appointments. There isn't a corner,
A moment, a shelf in the cupboard,
Or even a space in the cellar,
For phantoms and recollections.
There are too many words
For the past to be heard.
No one attends to the caller.

So mediums, goblins and revenants,
However well recommended
By curiosity, fate,
Guilt, or the S.P.R.,
No rapping on tables here:
No one's sufficiently bored.
Poltergeists, do not throw plates
To prove that you love us; and bogies,
Incubi, succubi, memories,
Get this in your empty heads —
You'll be ignored, ignored.
Leave us alone in our beds.
Go elsewhere, do not call here.

The Way Through the Woods

Rudyard Kipling

They shut the road through the woods
Seventy years ago.
Weather and rain have undone it again,
And now you would never know
There was once a road through the woods
Before they planted the trees.

It is underneath the coppice and heath,
And the thin anemones.
Only the keeper sees
That, where the ring-dove broods,
And the badgers roll at ease,
There was once a way through the woods.

Yet, if you enter the woods
Of a summer evening late,
When the night air cools on the trout-ringed pools
Where the otter whistles his mate,
(They fear not men in the woods,
Because they see so few)
You will hear the beat of a horse's feet,
And the swish of a skirt in the dew,
Steadily cantering through
The misty solitudes,
As though they perfectly knew
The old lost road through the woods . . .
But there is no road through the woods!

The 'Alice Jean'

Robert Graves

One moonlight night a ship drove in,
   A ghost ship from the west,
Drifting with bare mast and lone tiller;
   Like a mermaid drest
In long green weed and barnacles
   She beached and came to rest.

All the watchers of the coast
   Flocked to view the sight;
Men and women, streaming down
   Through the summer night,
Found her standing tall and ragged
   Beached in the moonlight.

Then one old woman stared aghast:
   'The *Alice Jean*? But no!
The ship that took my Ned from me
   Sixty years ago –
Drifted back from the utmost west
   With the ocean's flow?

'Caught and caged in the weedy pool
    Beyond the western brink,
Where crewless vessels lie and rot
    In waters black as ink,
Torn out at last by a sudden gale –
    Is it the *Jean*, you think?'

A hundred women gaped at her,
    The menfolk nudged and laughed,
But none could find a likelier story
    For the strange craft
With fear and death and desolation
    Rigged fore and aft.

The blind ship came forgotten home
    To all but one of these,
Of whom none dared to climb aboard her:
    And by and by the breeze
Veered hard about, and the *Alice Jean*
    Foundered in foaming seas.

Dicky

Robert Graves

Mother:
Oh what a heavy sigh!
    Dicky, are you ailing?

Dicky:
Even by the fireside, Mother,
    My heart is failing.

Tonight across the down,
    Whistling and jolly,
I sauntered out from town
    With my stick of holly.

Bounteous and cool from sea
    The wind was blowing,
Cloud shadows under the moon
    Coming and going.

I sang old country songs,
    Ran and leaped quick,
And turned home by St Swithin's
    Twirling my stick.

And there, as I was passing
    The churchyard gate,
An old man stopped me: 'Dicky,
    You're walking late.'

I did not know the man,
    I grew afeared
At his lean, lolling jaw,
    His spreading beard.

His garments old and musty,
    Of antique cut,
His body very frail and bony,
    His eyes tight shut.

Oh, even to tell it now
    My courage ebbs . . .
His face was clay, Mother,
    His beard cobwebs.

In that long horrid pause
    'Good night,' he said,
Entered and clicked the gate:
    'Each to his bed.'

Mother:
Do not sigh or fear, Dicky;
    How is it right
To grudge the dead their ghostly dark
    And wan moonlight?

We have the glorious sun,
    Lamp and fireside.
Grudge not the dead their moonbeams
    When abroad they ride.

The Choirmaster's Burial

Thomas Hardy

He often would ask us
That, when he died,
After playing so many
To their last rest,
If out of us any
Should here abide,
And it would not task us,
We would with our lutes
Play over him
By his grave-brim
The psalm he liked best —
The one whose sense suits
'Mount Ephraim' —
And perhaps we should seem
To him, in Death's dream,
Like the seraphim.

As soon as I knew
That his spirit was gone
I thought this his due,
And spoke thereupon.
'I think,' said the vicar,
'A read service quicker
Than viols out-of-doors
In these frosts and hoars.
That old-fashioned way
Requires a fine day,
And it seems to me
It had better not be.'

Hence, that afternoon,
Though never knew he
That his wish could not be,
To get through it faster
They buried the master
Without any tune.

But 'twas said that, when
At the dead of next night
The vicar looked out,
There struck on his ken
Thronged roundabout,

Where the frost was graying
The headstoned grass,
A band all in white
Like the saints in church-glass,
Singing and playing
The ancient stave
By the choirmaster's grave.

Such the tenor man told
When he had grown old.

The Last Wolf

Alastair W. Thomson

We killed at noon,
Where snow had withered from the yellow grass,
The last wolf in the hills.
Hounds circled in the wind, a horn
Blew to the crofts below.

The torn muzzle, the dark savaged fur,
Lay in the stillness like a trodden rug.
Whatever else, had gone
Out of the reach of axe or gun,
And had become
A black crag, or the wind.

We nailed the head
To a gnarled pear-tree by the wall;
Put up the guns, laid the axe by the wood-pile.
And under the rain, the melting spring,
It rotted slowly into bone;
White tusk of bone among the blossom
Of a warm spring, the land at peace.

Than such a blossom, nothing more.
Crops withered, udders dried;
The cobles found strange tides, but never fish,
And the wild berries only brought
The dry and dying land upon the tongue.

Now at the autumn's end
Black hail comes storming from the sea, beats down
The glens and valleys and the starving straths;
Wolf-weather, reiving snow.

The Witch

Gillian Pursey (aged 12)

The witch is an ugly creature.
Her clothes are tattered and torn.
She has hair as stiff as wire
And teeth as black as liquorice.
Her face has wrinkles like cracks in mountains.
Her lips are cold as stone.
Her eyes are like pebbles washed in a stream.
Her nose is sharp as a nail,
Her chin crooked like a twig.
Her fingers are like a spindly tree.
She laughs as she sails about on her broomstick
Because her feet are as big as boats.

The Hag

Robert Herrick

The Hag is astride,
This night for to ride;
The Devill and shee together:
Through thick, and through thin,
Now out, and then in,
Though ne'r so foule be the weather.

A Thorn or a Burr
She takes for a Spurre:
With a lash of a Bramble she rides now,
Through Brakes and through Bryars
O're Ditches and Mires,
She followes the Spirit that guides now.

No Beast, for his food,
Dares now range the wood;
But husht in his laire he lies lurking:
   While mischiefs, by these,
   On Land and on Seas,
At noone of Night are a working.

   The storme will arise,
   And trouble the skies;
This night, and more for the wonder,
   The ghost from the Tomb
   Affrighted shall come
Cal'd out by the clap of the Thunder

Will-O'-Wisp

John Clare

I've seen the midnight morris-dance of hell
On the black moors while thicker darkness fell,
Like dancing lamps or bounding balls of fire,
Now in and out, now up and down, now higher,
As though an unseen horseman in his flight
Flew swinging up and down a lamp alight;
Then fixed, as though it feared its end to meet,
It shone as lamps shine in a stilly street;
Then all at once it shot and danced anew,
Till mixed with darkness out of sight it grew.
The simple shepherd under fear's eclipse
Views the dread omens of these will-o'-wisps,
And thinks them haunting spirits of the earth
That shine where midnight murders had their birth;
With souls of midnight and with heads of fire
To him they shine, and bound o'er moor and mire,
Blazing like burning, crackling wisps of straw;
He sees and hears them, then with sudden awe
He pictures thieves with lanthorn light in hand,
That in lone spots for murder waiting stand.
Upon the meadow bridge's very wall
He sees a lanthorn stand, and pictures all
The muttered voices that derange his ears;
And when more near the spot, his sickening fears
See the imagined lanthorn, light and all,
Without a plash into the water fall,

And in one moment on his stifled sight
It blanks his hopes and sets his terrors right.
For furlongs off it simmers up and down,
A will-o'-wisp; and breathless to the town
He hastes, and hardly dares to catch his breath,
Existing like a doubt of life or death
Until the sight of houses cools his fears
And fireside voices greet his happy ears.
And then he rubs his hands beside the fire,
And quakes, and tells how over moor and mire
The jack-o'-lanthorn with his burning tails
Had like to led him; and he bites his nails
With very fear to think out how the blaze
Had like to cheat him into dangerous ways:
How that he thought he heard some people stand
As likely thieves with lanthorn in their hand,
When in a moment — yet he heard no fall —
Down went the lanthorn from the arches' wall
Into the flood; and on that brig alone
How his heart seemed as growing into stone.

Lollocks

Robert Graves

By sloth on sorrow fathered,
These dusty-featured Lollocks
Have their nativity in all disordered
Back of cupboard drawers.

They play hide and seek
Among collars and novels
And empty medicine bottles,
And letters from abroad
That never will be answered.

Every sultry night
They plague little children,
Gurgling from the cistern,
Humming from the air,
Skewing up the bed-clothes,
Twitching the blind.

When the imbecile agèd
Are over-long in dying
And the nurse drowses,
Lollocks come skipping
Up the tattered stairs
And are nasty together
In the bed's shadow.

The signs of their presence
Are boils on the neck,
Dreams of vexation suddenly recalled
In the middle of the morning,
Languor after food.

Men cannot see them,
Men cannot hear them,
Do not believe in them —
But suffer the more
Both in neck and belly.

Women can see them —
O those naughty wives
Who sit by the fireside
Munching bread and honey,
Watching them in mischief
From corners of their eyes,
Slyly allowing them to lick
Honey-sticky fingers.

Sovereign against Lollocks
Are hard broom and soft broom,
To well comb the hair,
To well brush the shoe,
And to pay every debt
As it falls due.

A Mermaiden

Thomas Hennell

Cast up on the Cornish coast (as reported), September 1934

Chilled with salt dew, tossed on dark waters deep,
Sailors and fishers loved her in their sleep,

And not a few would wed her in their dreams!
    Yet when, within their net, one autumn night
They felt and dragged her sliding weight, it seems
Star-sprinkled skies and phosphorescent light
On all the billows' tops, and on the net
Making a spider's-mesh of sparkles bright,
Dripping like pearls off her curled horse-tail hair –
Low-breathed they haul, and dunch! she's on the planks all
    right.

    What may be done with her can no man fathom, yet
Pretty as paint she starts, but tails so awkwardly.
Nor any of the crew will wish or dare
To take her home and, for their very lives,
To face again their daughters and their wives.

    No fishing-clouts will fit her quite, and all in vain
They put her out fried mackerel and hot tea.
Says one, 'Things being a turn of year
'We'll take ashore the maid, and at the church
'Of Lanteglos-by-Fowey, being near –
'Along with pilchards, breams, and perch,
'Fruit, turnips, autumn-flowers and marrows
'Which ornament the choir-stalls, piers, and rails
'And openings of pulpit narrow,
'Put her in window for the Harvest Show!'
    ' – Though folk will have to mind her dripping tails
'Upon their bonnets, hymn-books, shawls, and pews.
'I'll hurry to the Rector with the news
'And just remark "Look here, sir, what we've found!
'"Are we to drop her back, or in a tank
'"Send her along to the Aquarium?"'
'O-ho!' some others cried,
'We'll run her up the High-Street in a barrow.'

    An elder stroked his chin, and drank some rum
From wickered bottle: 'Nay, for did we so,
'Being a witch, she'd visit us with woe;
'Or nightmares foul or other sort of itch –
'She or some kindred doubtful spirit dumb!
' – She weeps and calls her lover, but in vain,
'These sea-maids marry none but sailors drowned,
'Fetch wind-spouts, or bring whirlpools in a calm!'
    With this, he smites one crab-fist down in palm,
'I'll just say what, we'll simply scrag the witch!
'And in the cauldron used for melting pitch

'Boil down the tail-end: she is every sailor's foe
'And simply lures poor duffers to their fate.
'The rest we'll cut in lumps and use for bait.'

On this, the boatswain rather sternly spoke:
'Friend, what you say goes farther than a joke.
''Twas honest counsel beyond any doubt,
'Yet did the parish constable find out,
'He and the clergyman would call it guilt:
'So might for her cold blood thy hot be spilt!'

   So then a more religious gave his mind:
''Twould be temptation to the village boys
'And frighten half the maids, if they should find
'That ladies such as this should be,
'Who may betroth the dead, or with a spirit
'Vex us, and what our children may inherit:
'And bring about, perhaps, our total loss.
'We being Christians, needs must sink her with the cross.'

   And so with spars and ropes they made her fast
And with the anchor sank. There, fathoms deep,
She found the sandy bottom, so for aye to sleep.

   Later near by they hung a passing bell
Hard by a charted rock: which tolls the rising swell.

Something Tapped

Thomas Hardy

Something tapped on the pane of my room
   When there was never a trace
Of wind or rain, and I saw in the gloom
   My weary Belovèd's face.

'O I am tired of waiting,' she said,
   'Night, morn, noon, afternoon;
So cold it is in my lonely bed,
   And I thought you would join me soon!'

I rose and neared the window-glass,
   But vanished thence had she:
Only a pallid moth, alas,
   Tapped at the pane for me.

The Wife of Usher's Well

Anon

There lived a wife at Usher's Well
   And a wealthy wife was she;
She had three stout and stalwart sons
   And sent them o'er the sea.

They hadna been a week from her,
   A week but barely ane,
Whan word came to the carlin wife   peasant
   That her three sons were gane.

They hadna been a week from her,
   A week but barely three,
Whan word came to the carlin wife
   That her sons she'd never see.

'I wish the wind may never cease,
   Nor fashes in the flood,   storms
Till my three sons come hame to me,
   In earthly flesh and blood.'

It fell about the Martinmass,
   When nights are lang and mirk,
The carlin wife's three sons came hame,
   And their hats were o' the birk.   birch

It neither grew in syke nor ditch,   brook
   Nor yet in ony sheugh;   ditch
But at the gates o' Paradise,
   That birk grew fair eneugh.

'Blow up the fire, my maidens!
   Bring water from the well!
For a' my house shall feast this night,
   Since my three sons are well.'

And she has made to them a bed,
   She's made it large and wide,
And she's ta'en her mantle her about,
   Sat down at the bed-side.

Up then crew the red, red cock,
    And up and crew the gray;
The eldest to the youngest said,
    "'Tis time we were away.'

The cock he hadna craw'd but once,
    And clapp'd his wings at a',
When the youngest to the eldest said,
    'Brother, we must awa'.

'The cock doth craw, the day doth daw,
    The channerin' worm doth chide;   gnawing
Gin we be mist out o' our place,
    A sair pain we maun bide.

'Fare ye weel, my mother dear!
    Fareweel to barn and byre!
And fare ye weel, the bonny lass
    That kindles my mother's fire!'

'Is my team ploughing?'

A. E. Housman

'Is my team ploughing,
    That I was used to drive
And hear the harness jingle
    When I was man alive?'

Ay, the horses trample,
    The harness jingles now;
No change though you lie under
    The land you used to plough.

'Is football playing
    Along the river shore,
With lads to chase the leather,
    Now I stand up no more?'

Ay, the ball is flying,
    The lads play heart and soul;
The goal stands up, the keeper
    Stands up to keep the goal.

'Is my girl happy,
    That I thought hard to leave,
And has she tired of weeping
    As she lies down at eve?'

Ay, she lies down lightly,
    She lies not down to weep:
Your girl is well contented.
    Be still, my lad, and sleep.

'Is my friend hearty,
    Now I am thin and pine,
And has he found to sleep in
    A better bed than mine?'

Yes, lad, I lie easy,
    I lie as lads would choose;
I cheer a dead man's sweetheart,
    Never ask me whose.

Enemies

Siegfried Sassoon

He stood alone in some queer sunless place
Where Armageddon ends. Perhaps he longed
For days he might have lived; but his young face
Gazed forth untroubled: and suddenly there thronged
Round him the hulking Germans that I shot
When for his death my brooding rage was hot.

He stared at them, half-wondering; and then
They told him how I'd killed them for his sake –
Those patient, stupid, sullen ghosts of men;
And still there seemed no answer he could make.
At last he turned and smiled. One took his hand
Because his face could make them understand.

Strange Meeting

Wilfred Owen

It seemed that out of battle I escaped
Down some profound dull tunnel, long since scooped
Through granites which titanic wars had groined.

Yet also there encumbered sleepers groaned,
Too fast in thought or death to be bestirred.
Then, as I probed them, one sprang up, and stared
With piteous recognition in fixed eyes,
Lifting distressful hands as if to bless.
And by his smile, I knew that sullen hall,
By his dead smile, I knew we stood in Hell.
With a thousand pains that vision's face was grained;
Yet no blood reached there from the upper ground,
And no guns thumped, or down the flues made moan.
'Strange friend,' I said, 'here is no cause to mourn.'
'None,' said that other, 'save the undone years,
The hopelessness. Whatever hope is yours,
Was my life also; I went hunting wild
After the wildest beauty in the world,
Which lies not calm in eyes, or braided hair,
But mocks the steady running of the hour,
And if it grieves, grieves richlier than here.
For of my glee might many men have laughed,
And of my weeping something had been left,
Which must die now. I mean the truth untold,
The pity of war, the pity war distilled.
Now men will go content with what we spoiled,
Or, discontent, boil bloody, and be spilled.
They will be swift with swiftness of the tigress.
None will break ranks though nations trek from progress.
Courage was mine and I had mystery,
Wisdom was mine, and I had mastery:
To miss the march of this retreating world
Into vain citadels that are not walled.
Then, when much blood had clogged their chariot-wheels,
I would go up and wash them from sweet wells,
Even with truths that lie too deep for taint.
I would have poured my spirit without stint
But not through wounds; not on the cess of war.
Foreheads of men have bled where no wounds were.
I am the enemy you killed, my friend.
I knew you in this dark: for so you frowned
Yesterday through me as you jabbed and killed.
I parried; but my hands were loath and cold.
Let us sleep now. . . .'

Lazarus

Elizabeth Jennings

It was the amazing white, it was the way he simply
Refused to answer our questions, it was the cold pale glance
Of death upon him, the smell of death that truly
Declared his rising to us. It was no chance
Happening, as a man may fill a silence
Between two heart-beats, seem to be dead and then
Astonish us with the closeness of his presence;
This man was dead, I say it again and again.
All of our sweating bodies moved towards him
And our minds moved too, hungry for finished faith.
He would not enter our world at once with words
That we might be tempted to twist or argue with:
Cold like a white root pressed in the bowels of earth
He looked, but also vulnerable — like birth.

St Martin and the Beggar

Thom Gunn

Martin sat young upon his bed
A budding cenobite,   monk
Said, 'Though I hold the principles
Of Christian life be right,
I cannot grow from them alone,
I must go out to fight.'

He travelled hard, he travelled far,
The light began to fail.
'Is not this act of mine,' he said,
'A cowardly betrayal,
Should I not peg my nature down
With a religious nail?'

Wind scudded on the marshland,
And, dangling at his side,
His sword soon clattered under hail:
What could he do but ride? —
There was not shelter for a dog,
The garrison far ahead.

A ship that moves on darkness
He rode across the plain,
When a brawny beggar started up
Who pulled at his rein
And leant dripping with sweat and water
Upon the horse's mane.

He glared into Martin's eyes
With eyes more wild than bold;
His hair sent rivers down his spine;
Like a fowl plucked to be sold
His flesh was grey. Martin said –
'What, naked in this cold?

'I have not food to give you,
Money would be a joke.'
Pulling his new sword from the sheath
He took his soldier's cloak
And cut it in two equal parts
With a single stroke.

Grabbing one to his shoulders,
Pinning it with his chin,
The beggar dived into the dark,
And soaking to the skin
Martin went on slowly
Until he reached an inn.

One candle on the wooden table,
The food and drink were poor,
The woman hobbled off, he ate,
Then casually before
The table stood the beggar as
If he had used the door.

Now dry for hair and flesh had been
By warm airs fanned,
Still bare but round each muscled thigh
A single golden band,
His eyes now wild with love, he held
The half cloak in his hand.

'You recognized the human need
Included yours, because
You did not hesitate, my saint,
To cut your cloak across;
But never since that moment
Did you regret the loss.

'My enemies would have turned away,
My holy toadies would
Have given all the cloak and frozen
Conscious that they were good.
But you, being a saint of men,
Gave only what you could.'

St Martin stretched his hand out
To offer from his plate,
But the beggar vanished, thinking food
Like cloaks is needless weight.
Pondering on the matter,
St Martin bent and ate.

Night and Dreams

Pigeons in flight. Photograph by Tom Biro.

Shadows

Peter Redgrove

'I do not say that shadows are a creature either, but I remember
When I saw them like this first:
A candle snapped its flare at shadows,
Fighting the six-inch fresh-air current to the door,
Flipped them into huddling corners:
They leapt up chairs and dangled from the ceiling,
Fattened there, dropped, swerved and ducked for cover.
A puff jabbing through the scratching curtains
Felled the flame, and with a lunge
They swept together close as eyelids on my cot.
I threw my only missile at the sightless,
And as the rattle scampered too and pattered,
Whipped back the half-silence, cowering with yells.
(But as I stopped for breath, I heard the night still scraping.)
Then my mother came in with another candle,
Her face bathed bleak-white and the flame blown back
And a wake of shadow-crowds tossing at her skirt.
She stooped and kissed me: gloom hollowed out her eyes;
(I do not say that shadows are a creature, but I
Sleep early too, wry-lidded to the pillow)
There were shadows to spare to tussle in my room:
And plenty left to go back with her, hanging on her face.'

Fear

Gillian Anderson (aged 15)

Walking through the park
Things deceive me in the dark.
Trees loom up on every side,
Make me feel I want to hide.
Shadows follow my every pace,
I feel my heart begin to race.
Can it be my mind at work
That I see creatures round me lurk?
I run for home as fast can be.
I'm sure that shadow was not a tree!

The Interned Refugee

W. R. Rodgers

And I was left here in the darkened house,
Listening for the fat click of the softly-shut door,
Looking for the oiled glint and ghost of light
Sliding soundlessly along the wall towards me,
Knowing that around me They were mobilizing
Their cold implacable forces slowly.

I shouted and none answered, one by one
My listening hopes crept back to me
Out of that dead place; mine was a lighted face
Looking into darkness, seen, but seeing nothing.

Banshee

Vernon Scannell

Interpreted by night
    This landscape alarms:
Not darkness but the icy light
    Which fixes and embalms.

The voices of the farms
    Are clubbed to silence, stilled;
Quiet now each appetite
    That bellowed, barked or shrilled.

Each cottage has been killed,
    Its eyes put out:
The corpse of noise is actual as
    A corporal shout:

As actual, in fact,
    As the stab in heart and bowel
When, suddenly, the moon lets out
    One long, despairing howl.

The Sentry

Alun Lewis

I have begun to die.
For now at last I know
That there is no escape
From Night. Not any dream
Nor breathless images of sleep
Touch my bat's-eyes. I hang
Leathery-arid from the hidden roof
Of Night, and sleeplessly
I watch within Sleep's province.
I have left
The lovely bodies of the boy and girl
Deep in each other's placid arms;
And I have left
The beautiful lanes of sleep
That barefoot lovers follow to this last
Cold shore of thought I guard.
I have begun to die
And the guns' implacable silence
Is my black interim, my youth and age,
In the flower of fury, the folded poppy,
Night.

The Nightwatchman

Peter Bland

I am the nightwatchman, left to face
The darkness you're afraid of
And which, long ago, I also dreaded,
Hiding my head beneath the blankets
For fear of faces reddened by hell's flames

As mine is now — but by the torch I carry
As warrant of my lonely trade.
While you are sleeping, I am seeing
The darker side of the gross machinery
That waits to claim you when my warrant fades.

I see it white-sheeted, cold, and idle,
Beneath black ribs of echoing steel.
I like to pretend it's a church I'm guarding —
Loose wires are moss beneath my feet
And lathes leap up like spires or vaulting.

Sometimes, alone in my cold cathedral,
I ask myself if I am ghost or priest
Or simply sole remnant of a congregation
That has long deserted — or lies asleep
Beneath these coils of shining weeds.

Perhaps I'm all of these — ghost, priest,
And congregation wrapped in one.
I have to believe there's some advantage
Left in facing what you're sleeping off.
Maybe I've been alone too long.

For I cannot imagine ever changing
My nightly passage for your kingdom come,
Nor could I face the thought of staying
With those ghosts that gather when I have gone
To lie beneath the blazing sun.

Night Crow

Theodore Roethke

When I saw that clumsy crow
Flap from a wasted tree,
A shape in the mind rose up:
Over the gulfs of dream
Flew a tremendous bird
Further and further away
Into a moonless black,
Deep in the brain, far back.

The Owl

Walter de la Mare

Owl of the wildwood I:
Muffled in sleep I drowse,
Where no fierce sun in heaven
Can me arouse.

My haunt's a hollow
In a half-dead tree,
Whose strangling ivy
Shields and shelters me,

But when dark's starlight
Thrids my green domain,
My plumage trembles and stirs,
I wake again:

A spectral moon
Silvers the world I see;
Out of their daylong lairs
Creep thievishly

Night's living things.
Then I,
Wafted away on soundless pinions
Fly;
Curdling her arches
With my hunting-cry:

A-hooh! a-hooh:
Four notes; and then,
Solemn, sepulchral, cold,
Four notes again,
The listening dingles
Of my woodland through:
A-hooh! A-hooh! —
  A-hooh!

The Owl

Edward Thomas

Downhill I came, hungry, and yet not starved;
Cold, yet had heat within me that was proof
Against the North wind; tired, yet so that rest
Had seemed the sweetest thing under a roof.

Then at the inn I had food, fire and rest,
Knowing how hungry, cold and tired was I.
All of the night was quite barred out except
An owl's cry, a most melancholy cry

Shaken out long and clear upon the hill,
No merry note, nor cause of merriment,
But one telling me plain what I escaped
And others could not, that night, as in I went.

And salted was my food, and my repose,
Salted and sobered, too, by the bird's voice
Speaking for all who lay under the stars,
Soldiers and poor, unable to rejoice.

Town Owl

Laurie Lee

On eves of cold, when slow coal fires,
rooted in basements, burn and branch,
brushing with smoke the city air;

When quartered moons pale in the sky,
and neons glow along the dark
like deadly nightshade on a briar;

Above the muffled traffic then
I hear the owl, and at his note
I shudder in my private chair.

For like an augur he has come
to roost among our crumbling walls,
his blooded talons sheathed in fur.

Some secret lure of time it seems
has called him from his country wastes
to hunt a newer wasteland here.

And where the candelabra swung
bright with the dancers' thousand eyes
now his black, hooded pupils stare,

And where the silk-shoed lovers ran
with dust of diamonds in their hair,
he opens now his silent wing,

And, like a stroke of doom, drops down,
and swoops across the empty hall,
and plucks a quick mouse off the stair . . .

The Bat

Theodore Roethke

By day the bat is cousin to the mouse.
He likes the attic of an ageing house.

His fingers make a hat about his head.
His pulse beat is so slow we think him dead.

He loops in crazy figures half the night
Among the trees that face the corner light.

But when he brushes up against a screen,
We are afraid of what our eyes have seen:

For something is amiss or out of place
When mice with wings can wear a human face.

Fear by Moonlight

Phoebe Hesketh

The bullion-moon tonight is profligate
Flinging her borrowed silver down the steps,
Chilling dark fields with bold reflected light.
I open an iron gate and feel her cold
Bright fingers under mine; it is a night
Bared of accustomed secrecy – the stream
Is floodlit, every pond an open eye.

Transfixed by the naked moon, all objects seem
More than themselves, like figures in a cave
Awakened to crystal of a new Glass Age.
In this reflected world alone I move –
I and the stream. Grass powders as I pass;
Thin mirrors crack below my clumsy feet,
And breath is twisted in a rope of fear.

Crouching beside the stream in alder-shade
A creature, hairy and hooded, nurses a gun;
This silent partnership in that dark place
Assaults the quiet; I cannot turn and run
But must plunge on; it is not I who pull
Puppet-strings to jerk my wooden feet.

Then fear is snatched away in a flare of light;
The rope unwinds, for I have been betrayed
By no more than a thorn bush in a shade.
Was it for this the prickling sweat and clutch
Of terror? Hell-Gate opened for a bush?
Moon, turn away your sun-reflecting face
And let me put the world back in its place.

Falling Asleep

Siegfried Sassoon

Voices moving about in the quiet house:
Thud of feet and a muffled shutting of doors:
Everyone yawning. Only the clocks are alert.

Out in the night there's autumn-smelling gloom
Crowded with whispering trees; across the park
A hollow cry of hounds like lonely bells:
And I know that the clouds are moving across the moon;
The low, red, rising moon. Now herons call
And wrangle by their pool; and hooting owls
Sail from the wood above pale stooks of oats.

Waiting for sleep, I drift from thoughts like these;
And where today was dream-like, build my dreams.
Music . . . there was a bright white room below,
And someone singing a song about a soldier,
One hour, two hours ago: and soon the song
Will be '*last night*': but now the beauty swings
Across my brain, ghost of remembered chords
Which still can make such radiance in my dream
That I can watch the marching of my soldiers,
And count their faces; faces; sunlit faces.

Falling asleep . . . the herons, and the hounds . . .
September in the darkness; and the world
I've known; all fading past me into peace.

Insomniac

Sylvia Plath

The night sky is only a sort of carbon paper,
Blueblack, with the much-poked periods of stars
Letting in the light, peephole after peephole –
A bonewhite light, like death, behind all things.
Under the eyes of the stars and the moon's rictus
He suffers his desert pillow, sleeplessness
Stretching its fine, irritating sand in all directions.

Over and over the old, granular movie
Exposes embarrassments – the mizzling days
Of childhood and adolescence, sticky with dreams,
Parental faces on tall stalks, alternately stern and tearful,
A garden of buggy roses that made him cry.
His forehead is bumpy as a sack of rocks.
Memories jostle each other for face-room like obsolete film stars.

He is immune to pills: red, purple, blue –
How they lit the tedium of the protracted evening!
Those sugary planets whose influence won for him
A life baptized in no-life for a while,
And the sweet, drugged waking of a forgetful baby.
Now the pills are wornout and silly, like classical gods.
Their poppy-sleepy colours do him no good.

His head is a little interior of grey mirrors.
Each gesture flees immediately down an alley
Of diminishing perspectives, and its significance
Drains like water out the hole at the far end.
He lives without privacy in a lidless room,
The bald slots of his eyes stiffened wide-open
On the incessant heat-lightning flicker of situations.

Nightlong, in the granite yard, invisible cats
Have been howling like women, or damaged instruments.
Already he can feel daylight, his white disease,
Creeping up with her hatful of trivial repetitions.
The city is a map of cheerful twitters now,
And everywhere people, eyes mica-silver and blank,
Are riding to work in rows, as if recently brainwashed.

Vigil

W. E. Henley

Lived on one's back,
In the long hours of repose
Life is a practical nightmare –
Hideous asleep or awake.

Shoulders and loins
Ache ——!
Ache, and the mattress,
Runs into boulders and hummocks,
Glows like a kiln, while the bedclothes –
Tumbling, importunate, daft –
Ramble and roll, and the gas,
Screwed to its lowermost,
An inevitable atom of light,
Haunts, and a stertorous sleeper
Snores me to hate and despair.

All the old time
Surges malignant before me;
Old voices, old kisses, old songs
Blossom derisive about me;
While the new days
Pass me in endless procession:
A pageant of shadows
Silently, leeringly wending
On . . . and still on . . . still on!

Far in the stillness a cat
Languishes loudly. A cinder
Falls and the shadows
Lurch to the leap of the flame. The next man to me
Turns with a moan; and the snorer,
The drug like a rope at his throat,
Gasps, gurgles, snorts himself free, as the night-nurse
Noiseless and strange,
Her bull's eye half-lanterned in apron,
(Whispering me, 'Are ye no sleepin' yet?')
Passes, list-slippered and peering,
Round . . . and is gone.

Sleep comes at last —
Sleep full of dreams and misgivings —
Broken with brutal and sordid
Voices and sounds that impose on me,
Ere I can wake to it,
The unnatural, intolerable day.

What Did I Dream?

Robert Graves

What did I dream? I do not know —
    The fragments fly like chaff.
Yet, strange, my mind was tickled so
    I cannot help but laugh.

Pull the curtains close again,
    Tuck me grandly in;
Must a world of humour wane
    Because birds begin

Complaining in a fretful tone,
    Rousing me from sleep —
The finest entertainment known,
    And given rag-cheap?

Drugged

Walter de la Mare

Inert in his chair,
In a candle's guttering glow;
His bottle empty,
His fire sunk low;
With drug-sealed lids shut fast,
Unsated mouth ajar,
This darkened phantasm walks
Where nightmares are:

In a frenzy of life and light,
Crisscross — a menacing throng —
They gibe, they squeal at the stranger,
Jostling along,
Their faces cadaverous grey:
While on high from an attic stare
Horrors, in beauty apparelled,
Down the dark air.

A stream gurgles over its stones,
The chambers within are afire.
Stumble his shadowy feet
Through shine, through mire;
And the flames leap higher.
In vain yelps the wainscot mouse;
In vain beats the hour;
Vacant, his body must drowse
Until daybreak flower —

Staining these walls with its rose,
And the draughts of the morning shall stir
Cold on cold brow, cold hands.
And the wanderer
Back to flesh house must return.
Lone soul — in horror to see,
Than dream more meagre and awful,
Reality.

The Nightmare

Elizabeth Jennings

The dream was that old falling one;
Sometimes it comes when, half-awake,
You drop down deep into the bed
And rouse yourself. The first sleeps break.

But this was further in the night.
I was upon a high trapeze,
Not in a circus but a street,
Myself the audience I must please.

And past and present met there in
The dangerous clarity dreams have.
I hated every detail yet
Saw all the world I swayed above.

I moved into a shallow doze
And not for hours could I convince
Myself that all this was a dream:
Nightmares can leave such finger-prints.

And, later still, I lived again,
As in an adolescent trance,
The terror of the acrobat.
And could all this be due to chance?

No doubt if I was laid upon
A doctor's couch, he soon would learn,
And teach to me, the meaning there,
And yet I'm sure I still would turn

Dizzy above the dizzy world.
I feel it sometimes now by day:
The streets I walk seem built of air
And all the solid houses sway.

Nightmare Song

W. S. Gilbert

When you're lying awake with a dismal headache and repose is
   tabooed by anxiety,
I conceive you may use any language you choose to indulge in
   without impropriety;
For your brain is on fire – the bedclothes conspire of your usual
   slumber to plunder you:
First your counterpane goes, and uncovers your toes, and your
   sheet slips demurely from under you;
Then the blanketing tickles – you feel like mixed pickles – so
   terribly sharp is the pricking,
And you're hot and you're cross, and you tumble and toss till
   there's nothing 'twixt you and the ticking.
Then the bedclothes all creep to the ground in a heap, and you
   pick 'em all up in a tangle;

Next your pillow resigns, and politely declines to remain at its usual angle!

Well, you get some repose in the form of a doze, with hot eyeballs and head ever aching,

But your slumbering teems with such horrible dreams that you'd very much better be waking:

For you dream you are crossing the Channel, and tossing about in a steamer from Harwich —

Which is something between a large bathing-machine and a very small second-class carriage —

And you're giving a treat (penny ice and cold meat) to a party of friends and relations —

They're a ravenous horde — and they all came on board at Sloane Square and South Kensington Stations.

And bound on that journey you find your attorney (who started that morning from Devon);

He's a bit undersized, and you don't feel surprised when he tells you he's only eleven.

Well, you're driving like mad with that singular lad (by the by, the ship's now a four-wheeler),

And you're playing round games, and he calls you bad names when you tell him that 'ties pay the dealer';

But this you can't stand, so you throw up your hand, and you find you're as cold as an icicle,

In your shirt and your socks (the black silk with gold clocks), crossing Salisbury Plain on a bicycle:

And he and the crew are on bicycles too — which they've somehow or other invested in —

And he's telling the tars all the particu*lars* of a company he's interested in —

It's a scheme of devices to get at low prices all goods from cough mixtures to cables

(Which tickled the sailors), by treating retailers as though they were all vege*ta*bles —

You get a good spadesman to plant a small tradesman (first take off his boots with a boot-tree),

And his legs will take root, and his fingers will shoot, and they'll blossom and bud like a fruit-tree —

From the greengrocer tree you get grapes and green pea, cauliflower, pineapple, and cranberries,

While the pastrycook plant, cherry brandy will grant, apple-puffs, and three-corners, and Banburys —

The shares are a penny, and ever so many are taken by Rothschild and Baring,

And just as a few are allotted to you, you awake with a shudder despairing —

You're a regular wreck with a crick in your neck, and no wonder you snore, for your head's on the floor, and you've needles and pins from your soles to your shins, and your flesh is a-creep, for your left leg's asleep, and you've cramp in your toes, and a fly in your nose, and some fluff in your lung, and a feverish tongue, and a thirst that's intense, and a general sense that you haven't been sleeping in clover;
But the darkness has past, and it's daylight at last, and the night has been long – ditto ditto my song – and thank goodness they're both of them over!

The Shadow of Night

Coventry Patmore

How strange it is to wake
   And watch while others sleep,
Till sight and hearing ache
   For objects that may keep
The awful inner sense
   Unroused, lest it should mark
The life that haunts the emptiness
   And horror of the dark.

How strange the distant bay
   Of dogs; how wild the note
Of cocks that scream for day,
   In homesteads far remote;
How strange and wild to hear
   The old and crumbling tower,
Amidst the darkness, suddenly
   Take life and speak the hour. . . .

The Sleepwalker

Antun Branko Simic (trans. Janko Lavrin)

The god of night
the moon
descends from heaven
and softly walks towards the house.

He climbs upon my window
and rests his eye on me
entices me into the night
I rise . . . and my white face . . . is smiling.

In sleep I step along the edges of the roof
and through the night I walk on high
The arms of the moon hold me aloft —

Light . . . unearthly . . . soaring
on a tree-leaf I could stand

But do not call: a voice from earth below
would kill my heavenly state
High above the earth I soar through the spheres.

Asleep

Wilfred Owen

Under his helmet, up against his pack,
After the many days of work and waking,
Sleep took him by the brow and laid him back.
And in the happy no-time of his sleeping,
Death took him by the heart. There was a quaking
Of the aborted life within him leaping . . .
Then chest and sleepy arms once more fell slack.
And soon the slow, stray blood came creeping
From the intrusive lead, like ants on track.

*   *   *

Whether his deeper sleep lie shaded by the shaking
Of great wings, and the thoughts that hung the stars,
High pillowed on calm pillows of God's making
Above these clouds, these rains, these sleets of lead,
And these winds' scimitars;
— Or whether yet his thin and sodden head
Confuses more and more with the low mould,
His hair being one with the grey grass
And finished fields of autumns that are old . . .
Who knows? Who hopes? Who troubles? Let it pass!
He sleeps. He sleeps less tremulous, less cold
Than we who must awake, and awaking, say Alas!

Conscious

Wilfred Owen

His fingers wake, and flutter; up the bed.
His eyes come open with a pull of will,
Helped by the yellow may-flowers by his head.
The blind-cord drawls across the window-sill . .
What a smooth floor the ward has! What a rug!
Who is that talking somewhere out of sight?
Why are they laughing? What's inside that jug?
'Nurse! Doctor!' – 'Yes; all right, all right.'

But sudden evening muddles all the air –
There seems no time to want a drink of water,
Nurse looks so far away. And here and there
Music and roses burst through crimson slaughter
He can't remember where he saw the blue sky.
More blankets. Cold. He's cold. And yet so hot.
And there's no light to see the voices by;
There is no time to ask – he knows not what.

The Ocean in London

Harold Monro

In London while I slowly wake
At morning I'm amazed to hear
The ocean, seventy miles away,
Below my window roaring, near.

When first I know that heavy sound
I keep my eyelids closely down,
And sniff the brine, and hold all thought
Reined back outside the walls of town.

So I can hardly well believe
That those tremendous billows are
Of iron and steel and wood and glass:
Van, lorry, and gigantic car.

Cock-Crow

Edward Thomas

Out of the wood of thoughts that grows by nigh
To be cut down by the sharp axe of light —
Out of the night, two cocks together crow,
Cleaving the darkness with a silver blow:
And bright before my eyes twin trumpeters stand,
Heralds of splendour, one at either hand,
Each facing each as in a coat of arms:
The milkers lace their boots up at the farms.

Wonders and Terrors
of the Mind

The Magnifying Glass

Walter de la Mare

With this round glass
I can make *Magic* talk –
A myriad shells show
In a scrap of chalk;

Of but an inch of moss
A forest – flowers and trees;
A drop of water
Like a hive of bees.

I lie in wait and watch
How the deft spider jets
The woven web-silk
From his spinnerets;

The tigerish claws he has!
And oh! the silly flies
That stumble into his net –
With all those eyes!

Not even the tiniest thing
But this my glass
Will make more marvellous,
And itself surpass.

Yes, and with lenses like it,
Eyeing the moon,
'Twould seem you'd walk there
In an afternoon!

ail from 'The Temptation of St. Antony' by Bosch.

Lost Love

Robert Graves

His eyes are quickened so with grief,
He can watch a grass or leaf
Every instant grow; he can
Clearly through a flint wall see,
Or watch the startled spirit flee
From the throat of a dead man.
   Across two counties he can hear
And catch your words before you speak.
The woodlouse or the maggot's weak
Clamour rings in his sad ear,
And noise so slight it would surpass
Credence – drinking sound of grass,
Worm talk, clashing jaws of moth
Chumbling holes in cloth;
The groan of ants who undertake
Gigantic loads for honour's sake
(Their sinews creak, their breath comes thin);
Whir of spiders when they spin,
And minute whisperings, mumblings, sighs
Of idle grubs and flies.
   This man is quickened so with grief
He wanders god-like or like thief
Inside and out, below, above,
Without relief seeking lost love.

Miracles

Walt Whitman

Why, who makes much of a miracle?
As to me I know of nothing else but miracles,
Whether I walk the streets of Manhattan,
Or dart my sight over the roofs of houses toward the sky,
Or wade with naked feet along the beach just in the edge of the
    water,
Or stand under trees in the woods,
Or talk by day with anyone I love, or sleep in the bed at night
    with anyone I love,
Or sit at table at dinner with the rest,
Or look at strangers opposite me riding in the car,
Or watch honey-bees busy around the hive of a summer fore-
    noon,
Or animals feeding in the fields,
Or birds, or the wonderfulness of insects in the air,
Or the wonderfulness of the sundown, or of stars shining so
    quiet and bright,
Or the exquisite delicate thin curve of the new moon in spring;
These with the rest, one and all, are to me miracles,
The whole referring, yet each distinct and in its place.

To me every hour of the light and dark is a miracle,
Every cubic inch of space is a miracle,
Every square yard of the surface of the earth is spread with the
    same,
Every foot of the interior swarms with the same.

To me the sea is a continual miracle,
The fishes that swim – the rocks – the motion of the waves – the
    ships with men in them,
What stranger miracles are there?

Rejectamenta

B. S. Johnson

In pieces, crockery acquires a beauty
that it did not have before; fragments
lie embedded in the clay, their colours
and shapes sudden and moving to the eye,
colours and shapes changed by weather and
the heat of ashes; this turquoise and primrose
floral border, for instance, would have seemed
unbearably trite complete, and willow
pattern excites (no piece like any other)
when broken up and scattered. Shattered roof-
tiles and flettons have weathered to a soft
warm ruddiness, and glass, green and clear,
glass, too, is changed: even a jamjar mouth
is beautiful after being splintered
by the weight of other rubbish, twisted
by the heat of clinker intermixed.

Clinker, ashes, leaves and branches mostly;
and batteries, bolts, oyster shells and cables,
rainpipe, a pair of scissors, a zipp fastener,
grinding wheels, a marble washstand top,
springs, fuse insulators, a metal drug
phial, some rubber hose, odd socks, a pair
of army boots laced together, a rusted
toy train, umbrella stays, and inner tubes;
a gas-mask filter, car parts, a soapdish,
torn coalsacks, slate, part of a tiled
surround, a teapot, switches and contacts,
a woman's shoe, the twisted spring of a
lever-arch file, film spools, a spatula,
and tins; for polish, cigarettes, sardines,
milk, talc, oil – these alone recognizable
by their shapes, the myriad other types
rusted into nonentity, the edge
corroding last of all; who was it said
the path of civilization is paved with tins?

Welsh Incident

Robert Graves

'But that was nothing to what things came out
From the sea-caves of Criccieth yonder.'
'What were they? Mermaids? dragons? ghosts?'
'Nothing at all of any things like that.'
'What were they, then?'
                              'All sorts of queer things,
Things never seen or heard or written about,
Very strange, un-Welsh, utterly peculiar
Things. Oh, solid enough they seemed to touch,
Had anyone dared it. Marvellous creation,
All various shapes and sizes, and no sizes,
All new, each perfectly unlike his neighbour,
Though all came moving slowly out together.'
'Describe just one of them.'
                              'I am unable.'
'What were their colours?'
                              'Mostly nameless colours
Colours you'd like to see; but one was puce
Or perhaps more like crimson, but not purplish.
Some had no colour.'
                      'Tell me, had they legs?'
'Not a leg nor foot among them that I saw.'
'But did these things come out in any order?
What o'clock was it? What was the day of the week?
Who else was present? How was the weather?'
'I was coming to that. It was half past three
On Easter Tuesday last. The sun was shining.
The Harlech Silver Band played *Marchog Jesu*
On thirty-seven shimmering instruments,
Collecting for Caernarvon's (Fever) Hospital Fund.
The populations of Pwllheli, Criccieth,
Portmadoc, Borth, Tremadoc, Penrhyndeudraeth,
Were all assembled. Criccieth's mayor addressed them
First in good Welsh and then in fluent English,
Twisting his fingers in his chain of office,
Welcoming the things. They came out on the sand,
Not keeping time to the band, moving seaward
Silently at a snail's pace. But at last
The most odd, indescribable thing of all,
Which hardly one man there could see for wonder,
Did something recognizably a something.'

'Well, what?'
                  'It made a noise.'
                                'A frightening noise?
'No, no.'
               'A musical noise? A noise of scuffling?'
'No, but a very loud, respectable noise –
Like groaning to oneself on Sunday morning
In Chapel, close before the second psalm.'
'What did the mayor do?'
                              'I was coming to that.'

The Tantanoola Tiger

Max Harris

There in the bracken was the ominous spoor mark,
Huge, splayed, deadly, and quiet as breath,
And all around lay bloodied and dying,
Staring dumbly into their several eternities,
The rams that Mr Morphett loved as sons.

Not only at Tantanoola, but at Mount Schank
The claw welts patterned the saplings
With mysteries terrible as Egypt's demons,
More evil than the blueness of the Lakes,
And less than a mile from the homestead, too.

Sheep died more rapidly than the years
Which the tiger rules in tooth and talk,
And it padded from Beachport to the Border,
While blood streamed down the minds of the folk
Of Mount Gambier, Tantanoola, and Casterton.

Oh this tiger was seen all right, grinning,
Yellow and gleaming with satin stripes:
Its body arched and undulated through the tea-tree:
In this land of dead volcanoes it was a flame.
It was a brightness, it was the glory of death:

It was fine, this tiger, a sweet shudder
In the heath and everlastings of the Border,
A roc bird up the ghostly ring-barked gums
Of Mingbool Swamp, a roaring fate
Descending on the mindless backs of grazing things.

Childhoods burned with its burning eyes,
Tantanoola was a magic playground word,
It rushed through young dreams like a river,
And it had lovers in Mr Morphett and Mr Marks
For the ten long hunting unbelieving years.

Troopers and blacks made safari, Africa-fashion;
Pastoral Quixotes swayed on their ambling mounts,
Lost in invisible trails. The red-faced
Young Lindsay Gordons of the Mount
Tormented their heartbeats in the rustling nights

While the tiger grew bigger, and clear as an axe.
'A circus once abandoned a tiger cub' —
This was the creed of the hunters and poets:
'A dingo that's got itself too far south'
The grey old cynics thundered in their beers;

And blows were swapped and friendships broken;
Beauty burst on a loveless and dreary people,
And their monied minds broke into singing
A myth; these soured and tasteless settlers
Were Greeks and Trojans, billabong troubadours,

Plucking their themes at the picnic races
Around the kegs in the flapping canvas booths.
On the waistcoats sharks' teeth swung in time,
And old eyes, sharply seamed and squinting,
Opened mysteriously in misty musical surprise,

Until the day Jack Heffernan made camp
By a mob of sheep on the far slope of Mount Schank,
And woke to find the tiger on its haunches,
Bigger than a mountain lion, love, or imagination,
Grinning lazily down on a dying ewe;

And he drew a bead and shot it through the head.
Look down, oh mourners of history, poets,
Look down on the black and breeding volcanic soil,
Lean on your fork in this potato country,
Regard the yellowed fangs and quivering claws

Of a mangy and dying Siberian wolf.
It came as a fable or a natural image
To pace the bars of those sunless minds,
A small and unimpressive common wolf
In desperately poor and cold condition.

It howled to the wattle when it swam ashore
From the wreck of the foundered *Helena*,
Smelt death and black snakes and tight lips
On every fence-post and slip-rail.
It was three foot six from head to tail.

Centuries will die like swatted blowflies
Before word of wolf will work a tremor
Of tenderness in the crusty knuckles
Around the glasses in the Tantanoola pub
Where its red bead eyes now stare towards the sun.

Digging for China

Richard Wilbur

'Far enough down is China,' somebody said.
'Dig deep enough and you might see the sky
As clear as at the bottom of a well.
Except it would be real — a different sky.
Then you could burrow down until you came
To China! Oh, it's nothing like New Jersey.
There's people, trees, and houses, and all that,
But much, much different. Nothing looks the same.

I went and got the trowel out of the shed
And sweated like a coolie all that morning,
Digging a hole beside the lilac-bush,
Down on my hands and knees. It was a sort
Of praying, I suspect. I watched my hand
Dig deep and darker, and I tried and tried
To dream a place where nothing was the same.
The trowel never did break through to blue.

Before the dream could weary of itself
My eyes were tired of looking into darkness,
My sunbaked head of hanging down a hole.
I stood up in a place I had forgotten,
Blinking and staggering while the earth went round
And showed me silver barns, the fields dozing
In palls of brightness, patens growing and gone   plates
In the tides of leaves, and the whole sky china blue.
Until I got my balance back again
All that I saw was China, China, China.

The Shell

James Stephens

I

And then I pressed the shell
Close to my ear,
And listened well.

And straightway, like a bell,
Came low and clear
The slow, sad, murmur of far distant seas

Whipped by an icy breeze
Upon a shore
Wind-swept and desolate.

It was a sunless strand that never bore
The footprint of a man,
Nor felt the weight

Since time began
Of any human quality or stir,
Save what the dreary winds and wave incur.

II

And in the hush of waters was the sound
Of pebbles, rolling round;
For ever rolling, with a hollow sound:

And bubbling sea-weeds, as the waters go
Swish to and fro
Their long cold tentacles of slimy grey:

There was no day;
Nor ever came a night
Setting the stars alight

To wonder at the moon:
Was twilight only, and the frightened croon,
Smitten to whimpers, of the dreary wind

And waves that journeyed blind . . .
And then I loosed an ear — Oh, it was sweet
To hear a cart go jolting down the street.

Healing a Lunatic Boy

Charles Causley

Trees turned and talked to me,
Tigers sang,
Houses put on leaves,
Water rang.
Flew in, flew out
On my tongue's thread
A speech of birds
From my hurt head.

At my fine lion
Fire and cloud kissed,
Rummaged the green bone
Beneath my wrist.
I saw a sentence
Of fern and tare
Write with loud light
The mineral air.

On a stopped morning
The city spoke,
In my rich mouth
Oceans broke.
No more on the spun shore
I walked unfed.
I drank the sweet sea,
Stones were bread.

Then came the healer
Grave as grass,
His hair of water
And hands of glass.
I watched at his tongue
The white words eat,
In death, dismounted
At his stabbed feet.

Now river is river
And tree is tree,
My house stands still
As the northern sea.
On my hundred of parables
I heard him pray,
Seize my smashed world,
Wrap it away.

Now the pebble is sour,
The birds beat high,
The fern is silent,
The river dry.
A seething summer
Burned to bone
Feeds at my mouth
But finds a stone.

Mental Cases

Wilfred Owen

Who are these? Why sit they here in twilight?
Wherefore rock they, purgatorial shadows,
Drooping tongues from jaws that slob their relish,
Baring teeth that leer like skulls' teeth wicked?
Stroke on stroke of pain — but what slow panic,
Gouged these chasms round their fretted sockets?
Ever from their hair and through their hands' palms
Misery swelters. Surely we have perished
Sleeping, and walk hell; but who these hellish?

— These are men whose minds the Dead have ravished.
Memory fingers in their hair of murders,
Multitudinous murders they once witnessed.
Wading sloughs of flesh these helpless wander,
Treading blood from lungs that had loved laughter.
Always they must see these things and hear them,
Batter of guns and shatter of flying muscles,
Carnage incomparable, and human squander
Rucked too thick for these men's extrication.

Therefore still their eyeballs shrink tormented
Back into their brains, because on their sense
Sunlight seems a blood-smear; night comes blood-black;
Dawn breaks open like a wound that bleeds afresh.
— Thus their heads wear this hilarious, hideous,
Awful falseness of set-smiling corpses.
— Thus their hands are plucking at each other;
Picking at the rope-knouts of their scourging;
Snatching after us who smote them, brother,
Pawing us who dealt them war and madness.

Gunpowder Plot

Vernon Scannell

For days these curious cardboard buds have lain
In brightly coloured boxes. Soon the night
Will come. We pray there'll be no sullen rain
To make these magic orchids flame less bright.

Now in the garden's darkness they begin
To flower: the frenzied whizz of Catherine-wheel
Puts forth its fiery petals and the thin
Rocket soars to burst upon the steel

Bulwark of a cloud. And then the guy,
Absurdly human phoenix, is again
Gulped by greedy flames: the harvest sky
Is flecked with threshed and glittering golden grain.

'Uncle! A cannon! Watch me as I light it!'
The women helter-skelter, squealing high,
Retreat; the paper fuse is quickly lit,
A cat-like hiss, and spit of fire, a sly

Falter, then the air is shocked with blast.
The cannon bangs and in my nostrils drifts
A bitter scent that brings the lurking past
Lurching to my side. The present shifts,

Allows a ten-year memory to walk
Unhindered now; and so I'm forced to hear
The banshee howl of mortar and the talk
Of men who died, am forced to taste my fear.

I listen for a moment to the guns,
The torn earth's grunts, recalling how I prayed.
The past retreats. I hear a corpse's sons —
'Who's scared of bangers!' 'Uncle! John's afraid!'

The Scene of War: Fear

Herbert Read

Fear is a wave
Beating through the air
And on taut nerves impinging
Till there it wins
Vibrating chords.

All goes well
So long as you tune the instrument
To simulate composure.

(So you will become
A gallant gentleman.)

But when the strings are broken. . . .
Then you will grovel on the earth
And your rabbit eyes
Will fill with the fragments of your shattered soul.

Suicide in the Trenches

Siegfried Sassoon

I knew a simple soldier boy
Who grinned at life in empty joy,
Slept soundly through the lonesome dark,
And whistled early with the lark.

In winter trenches, cowed and glum,
With crumps and lice and lack of rum,
He put a bullet through his brain.
No one spoke of him again.

                *   *   *

You smug-faced crowds with kindling eye
Who cheer when soldier lads march by,
Sneak home and pray you'll never know
The hell where youth and laughter go.

Solitude

Walter de la Mare

When the high road
Forks into a by-road,
And then drifts into a lane,
And the lane breaks into a bridle-path,
A chace forgotten
Still as death,
And green with the long night's rain;
Through a forest winding on and on,
Moss, and fern, and sun-bleached bone,
Till only a trace remains;
And that dies out in a waste of stone
A bluff or cliff, vast, trackless, wild,
Blue with the harebell, undefiled;
Where silence enthralls the empty air,
Mute with a presence unearthly fair,
And a path is sought
In vain . . .

It is then the Ocean
Looms into sight,
A gulf enringed with burning white,
A sea of sapphire, dazzling bright;
And islands
Peaks of such beauty that
Bright danger seems to lie in wait,
Dread, disaster, boding fate;
And soul and sense are appalled thereat;
Though an Ariel music on the breeze
Thrills the mind with a lorn unease,
Cold with all mortal mysteries.
And every thorn,
And weed, and flower,
And every time-worn stone
A challenge cries on the trespasser;
   Beware!
   Thou art alone!

The Black Peak

(*from 'The Prelude'*)

William Wordsworth

One summer evening . . . I found
A little boat tied to a willow-tree
Within a rocky cave, its usual home.
Straight I unloosed her chain, and stepping in
Pushed from the shore. It was an act of stealth
And troubled pleasure, nor without the voice
Of mountain echoes did my boat move on;
Leaving behind her still, on either side,
Small circles glittering idly in the moon,
Until they melted all into one track
Of sparkling light. But now, like one who rows,
Proud of his skill, to reach a chosen point
With an unswerving line, I fixed my view
Upon the summit of a craggy ridge,
The horizon's utmost boundary; far above
Was nothing but the stars and the grey sky.
She was an elfin pinnace; lustily
I dipped my oars into the silent lake,
And, as I rose upon the stroke, my boat
Went heaving through the water like a swan;
When, from behind that craggy steep till then
The horizon's bound, a huge peak, black and huge,
As if with voluntary power instinct
Upreared its head. I struck and struck again,
And growing still in stature the grim shape
Towered up between me and the stars, and still,
For so it seemed, with purpose of its own
And measured motion like a living thing,
Strode after me. With trembling oars I turned,
And through the silent water stole my way
Back to the covert of the willow-tree;
There in her mooring-place I left my bark,
And through the meadows homeward went, in grave
And serious mood; but after I had seen
That spectacle, for many days, my brain
Worked with a dim and undetermined sense
Of unknown modes of being; o'er my thoughts
There hung a darkness, call it solitude
Or blank desertion. No familiar shapes
Remained, no pleasant images of trees,
Of sea or sky, no colours of green fields;

But huge and mighty forms, that do not live
Like living men, moved slowly through the mind
By day, and were a trouble to my dreams.

The Fear

Andrew Young

How often I turn round
To face the beast that bound by bound
Leaps on me from behind,
Only to see a bough that heaves
With sudden gust of wind
Or blackbird raking withered leaves.

A dog may find me out
Or badger toss a white-lined snout;
And one day as I softly trod
Looking for nothing stranger than
A fox or stoat I met a man
And even that seemed not too odd.

And yet in any place I go
I watch and listen as all creatures do
For what I cannot see or hear,
For something warns me everywhere
That even in my land of birth
I trespass on the earth.

Haunted

Siegfried Sassoon

Evening was in the wood, louring with storm.
A time of drought had sucked the weedy pool
And baked the channels; birds had done with song.
Thirst was a dream of fountains in the moon,
Or willow-music blown across the water
Leisurely sliding on by weir and mill.

Uneasy was the man who wandered, brooding,
His face a little whiter than the dusk.
A drone of sultry wings flicker'd in his head.
The end of sunset burning thro' the boughs
Died in a smear of red; exhausted hours
Cumber'd, and ugly sorrows hemmed him in.

He thought: 'Somewhere there's thunder,' as he strove
To shake off dread; he dared not look behind him,
But stood, the sweat of horror on his face.

He blunder'd down a path, trampling on thistles,
In sudden race to leave the ghostly trees.
And: 'Soon I'll be in open fields,' he thought,
And half remembered starlight on the meadows,
Scent of mown grass and voices of tired men,
Fading along the field-paths; home and sleep
And cool-swept upland spaces, whispering leaves,
And far off the long churring night-jar's note.

But something in the wood, trying to daunt him,
Led him confused in circles through the thicket.
He was forgetting his old wretched folly,
And freedom was his need; his throat was choking.
Barbed brambles gripped and clawed him round his legs,
And he floundered over snags and hidden stumps.
Mumbling: 'I will get out! I must get out!'
Butting and thrusting up the baffling gloom,
Pausing to listen in a space 'twixt thorns,
He peers around with peering, frantic eyes.

An evil creature in the twilight looping,
Flapped blindly in his face. Beating it off,
He screeched in terror, and straightway something clambered
Heavily from an oak, and dropped, bent double,
To shamble at him zigzag, squat and bestial.

Headlong he charges down the wood, and falls
With roaring brain – agony – the snap't spark –
And blots of green and purple in his eyes.
Then the slow fingers groping on his neck,
And at his heart the strangling clasp of death.

The Trap

Jon Stallworthy

The first night that the monster lurched
Out of the forest on all fours,
He saw its shadow in his dream
Circle the house, as though it searched
For one it loved or hated. Claws
On gravel and a rabbit's scream
Ripped the fabric of his dream.

Waking between dark and dawn
And sodden sheets, his reason quelled
The shadow and the nightmare sound.
The second night it crossed the lawn
A brute voice in the darkness yelled.
He struggled up, woke raving, found
His wall-flowers trampled to the ground.

When rook wings beckoned the shadows back
He took his rifle down, and stood
All night against the leaded glass.
The moon ticked round. He saw the black
Elm-skeletons in the doomsday wood,
The sailing and the failing stars
And red coals dropping between bars.

The third night such a putrid breath
Fouled, flared his nostrils, that he turned,
Turned, but could not lift, his head.
A coverlet as thick as death
Oppressed him: he crawled out: discerned
Across the door his watchdog, dead.
'Build a trap,' the neighbours said.

All that day he built his trap
With metal jaws and a spring as thick
As the neck of a man. One touch
Triggered the hanging teeth: jump, snap,
And lightning guillotined the stick
Thrust in its throat. With gun and torch
He set his engine in the porch.

The fourth night in their beds appalled
His neighbours heard the hunting roar
Mount, mount to an exultant shriek.
At daybreak timidly they called
His name, climbed through the splintered door
And found him sprawling in the wreck,
Naked, with a severed neck.

The Wolves

Allen Tate

There are wolves in the next room waiting
With heads bent low, thrust out, breathing
At nothing in the dark; between them and me
A white door patched with light from the hall
Where it seems never (so still is the house)
A man has walked from the front door to the stair.
It has all been forever. Beasts claw the floor.
I have brooded on angels and archfiends
But no man has ever sat where the next room's
Crowded with wolves, and for the honour of man
I affirm that never have I before. Now while
I have looked for the evening star at a cold window
And whistled when Arcturus split his light,
I've heard the wolves scuffle, and said: So this
Is man; so — what better conclusion is there —
The day will not follow night, and the heart
Of man has a little dignity, but less patience
Than a wolf's, and a duller sense that cannot
Smell its own mortality. (This and other
Meditations will be suited to other times
After dog silence howls his epitaph.)
Now remember courage, go to the door,
Open it and see whether coiled on the bed
Or cringing by the wall, a savage beast
Maybe with golden hair, with deep eyes
Like a bearded spider on a sunlit floor
Will snarl — and man can never be alone.

Mushrooms

Sylvia Plath

Overnight, very
Whitely, discreetly,
Very quietly

Our toes, our noses
Take hold on the loam,
Acquire the air.

Nobody sees us,
Stops us, betrays us;
The small grains make room

Soft fists insist on
Heaving the needles,
The leafy bedding,

Even the paving,
Our hammers, our rams,
Earless and eyeless,

Perfectly voiceless,
Widen the crannies,
Shoulder through holes. We

Diet on water,
On crumbs of shadow,
Bland-mannered, asking

Little or nothing.
So many of us!
So many of us!

We are shelves, we are
Tables, we are meek,
We are edible,

Nudgers and shovers
In spite of ourselves.
Our kind multiplies:

We shall by morning
Inherit the earth.
Our foot's in the door.

Bedtime Story

George MacBeth

A giant ant is telling a bedtime story to one of its children. The story is the legend of how the last man was accidentally wiped out by a Mission Patrol wishing to help him. — *Author's note.*

Long long ago when the world was a wild place
Planted with bushes and peopled by apes, our
Mission Brigade was at work in the jungle.
    Hard by the Congo

Once, when a foraging detail was active
Scouting for green-fly, it came on a grey man, the
Last living man, in the branch of a baobab
    Stalking a monkey.

Earlier men had disposed of, for pleasure,
Creatures whose names we scarcely remember —
Zebra, rhinoceros, elephants, wart-hog,
    Lion, rats, deer. But

After the wars had extinguished the cities
Only the wild ones were left, half-naked
Near the Equator: and here was the last one,
    Starved for a monkey.

By then the Mission Brigade had encountered
Hundreds of such men: and their procedure,
History tells us, was only to feed them:
    Find them and feed them;

Those were the orders. And this was the last one.
Nobody knew that he was, but he was. Mud
Caked on his flat grey flanks. He was crouched, half-
    armed with a shaved spear

Glinting beneath broad leaves. When their jaws cut
Swathes through the bark and he saw fine teeth shine,
Round eyes roll round and forked arms waver
    Huge as the rough trunks

Over his head, he was frightened. Our workers
Marched through the Congo before he was born, but
This was the first time perhaps that he'd seen one.
    Staring in hot still

Silence, he crouched there: then jumped. With a long swing
Down from his branch, he had angled his spear too
Quickly, before they could hold him, and hurled it
　　Hard at the soldier

Leading the detail. How could he know Queen's
Orders were only to help him? The soldier
Winced when the tipped spear pricked him. Unsheathing his
　　Sting was a reflex.

Later the Queen was informed. There were no more
Men. An impetuous soldier had killed off,
Purely by chance, the penultimate primate.
　　When she was certain,

Squadrons of workers were fanned through the Congo
Detailed to bring back the man's pickled bones to be
Sealed in the archives in amber. I'm quite sure
　　Nobody found them

After the most industrious search, though.
Where had the bones gone? Over the earth, dear,
Ground by the teeth of the termites, blown by the
　　Wind, like the dodo's.

To Penetrate That Room

John Lehmann

To penetrate that room is my desire,
The extreme attic of the mind, that lies
Just beyond the last bend in the corridor.
Writing I do it. Phrases, poems are keys.
Loving's another way (but not so sure).
A fire's in there, I think, there's truth at last
Deep in a lumber chest. Sometimes I'm near,
But draughts puff out the matches, and I'm lost.
Sometimes I'm lucky, find a key to turn,
Open an inch or two – but always then
A bell rings, someone calls, or cries of 'fire'
Arrest my hand when nothing's known or seen,
And running down the stairs again I mourn.

To End her Fear

John Freeman

Be kind to her
O Time.
She is too much afraid of you
  Because yours is a land unknown,
  Wintry, dark and lone.

'Tis not for her
To pass
Boldly upon your roadless waste.
  Roads she loves, and the bright ringing
  Of quick heels, and clear singing.

She is afraid
Of Time,
Forty to seventy sadly fearing . . .
  O, all those unknown years,
  And these sly, stoat-like fears!

Shake not on her
Your snows,
But on the rich, the proud, the wise
  Who have that to make them glow
  With warmth beneath the snow.

If she grow old
At last,
  Be it yet unknown to her; that she
  Not until her last prayer is prayed
  May whisper, 'I am afraid!'

Start not!

Emily Brontë

Start not! upon the minster-wall
Sunshine is shed in holy calm;
And, lonely though my footsteps fall,
The saints shall shelter thee from harm.

Shrink not if it be summer noon –
This shadow should night's welcome be.
These stairs are steep, but landed soon
We'll rest us long and quietly.

What though our path be o'er the dead?
They slumber soundly in the tomb;
And why should mortals fear to tread
The pathway to their future home?

Prospice

Robert Browning

Fear death? – to feel the fog in my throat,
    The mist in my face,
When the snows begin, and the blasts denote
    I am nearing the place,
The power of the night, the press of the storm,
    The post of the foe;
Where he stands, the Arch Fear in a visible form,
    Yet the strong man must go:
For the journey is done and the summit attained,
    And the barriers fall,
Though a battle's to fight ere the guerdon be gained,
    The reward of it all.
I was ever a fighter, so – one fight more,
    The best and the last!
I would hate that death bandaged my eyes, and forebore,
    And bade me creep past.
No! let me taste the whole of it, fare like my peers
    The heroes of old,
Bear the brunt, in a minute pay glad life's arrears
    Of pain, darkness and cold.
For sudden the worst turns the best to the brave,
    The black minute's at end,
And the elements' rage, the fiend-voices that rave,
    Shall dwindle, shall blend,
Shall change, shall become first a peace out of pain,
    Then a light, then thy breast,
O thou soul of my soul! I shall clasp thee again,
    And with God be the rest!

A Hymne to God the Father

John Donne

Wilt thou forgive that sinne where I begunne,
    Which is my sin, though it were done before?
Wilt thou forgive those sinnes, through which I runne,
    And do run still: though still I do deplore?
        When thou hast done, thou hast not done,
           For, I have more.

Wilt thou forgive that sinne by which I'have wonne
    Others to sinne? and, made my sinne their doore?
Wilt thou forgive that sinne which I did shunne
    A yeare or two: but wallowed in, a score?
        When thou hast done, thou hast not done,
           For I have more.

I have a sinne of feare, that when I have spunne
    My last thred, I shall perish on the shore;
Sweare by thy selfe, that at my death thy sonne
    Shall shine as he shines now, and heretofore;
        And, having done that, Thou haste done,
           I feare no more.